# THE CHILTERNS YEAR ROUND WALKS

**Spring, Summer, Autumn & Winter**

## Ruth Paley

COUNTRYSIDE BOOKS
NEWBURY BERKSHIRE

First published 2018
Text © 2018 Ruth Paley

All rights reserved. No part of this publication may be reproduced, stored in a retrieval system, or transmitted by any means, electronic, mechanical, photocopying, recording or otherwise, without the prior written permission of the copyright holder and publishers.

COUNTRYSIDE BOOKS
3 Catherine Road
Newbury
Berkshire

To view our complete range of books please visit us at
www.countrysidebooks.co.uk

ISBN 978 1 84674 363 4

Photographs by Ruth Paley

Produced by The Letterworks Ltd., Reading
Typeset by KT Designs, St Helens
Printed by Holywell Press, Oxford

# Contents

Introduction

## Spring

1. **Cowleaze Wood and Aston Rowant Nature Reserve** ........... *Spring* ........ 7
   3 miles / 4.8km

2. **Wendover Canal and Woods** ................................................ *Spring* ...... 12
   7 miles / 11.2km

3. **Bradenham Estate** ................................................................. *Spring* ...... 17
   3 miles / 4.8km

4. **Hughenden Valley** ................................................................. *Spring* ...... 21
   4.5 miles / 7.2km

5. **Hailey and Ipsden** ................................................................. *Spring* ...... 25
   3.5 miles / 5.6km

## Summer

6. **Princes Risborough and Whiteleaf Cross** ........................... *Summer* ... 29
   7 miles / 11.2km

7. **Radnage to Lodge Hill** .......................................................... *Summer* ... 34
   4.5 miles / 7.2km

8. **Coombe Hill and Beacon Hill** ................................................ *Summer* ... 39
   7 miles / 11.2km

9. **Chenies and the Chess Valley** .............................................. *Summer* ... 44
   6 miles / 9.6km

10. **Hambleden Valley** ................................................................. *Summer* ... 48
    6.5 miles / 10.4km

# Contents

## Autumn

**11** Ashridge Estate .................................................................. *Autumn* ... 52
6.8 miles / 10.9km

**12** Aldbury and the Grand Union Canal ................................ *Autumn* ... 56
9 miles / 14.4km

**13** Nettlebed .......................................................................... *Autumn* ... 61
3 miles / 4.8km

**14** Burnham Beeches .............................................................. *Autumn* ... 65
3 miles / 4.8km

**15** Henley-on-Thames ............................................................. *Autumn* .. 69
8 miles / 12.8km

## Winter

**16** Goring and the Thames Path ............................................... *Winter* ..... 74
4 miles / 6.4km

**17** The Lee and Lee Common .................................................. *Winter* ..... 78
3 miles / 4.8km

**18** Medmenham and the River Thames ................................... *Winter* ..... 83
3 miles / 4.8km

**19** Bourne End and Spade Oak Lake ....................................... *Winter* ..... 87
3 miles / 4.8km

**20** Christmas Common ............................................................ *Winter* ..... 91
3 miles / 4.8km

# *Introduction*

Time spent outdoors is the best way to boost your mood and energy levels, at any time of year. The summer might seem the obvious time to head out for a walk, but there's nothing like a brisk stroll on a crisp winter's day, particularly when there's the twinkling lights of a village pub, with its beams and smoking fires, to welcome you back at the end of a good walk. And if you have got wet and cold on top of a Chiltern hill, then it will make getting warm and dry by a log fire all the more pleasurable.

Of course, before setting out in any season, remember the words of the wonderful Alfred Wainwright, "There's no such thing as bad weather, only unsuitable clothing." Slipping and sliding along a muddy bridleway with the water seeping into your boots is a situation no-one wants to find themselves in, and I think a year-round walker should never leave the house without a reliable pair of waterproof walking shoes.

In spring, the countryside comes alive, with the bleating of lambs in the fields, while woodland floors are magically carpeted with bluebells, wood anemone and celandine, and the hedgerows light up with the blossom of whitebeam and hawthorn. Beechwoods create the perfect habitat for bluebells, and there are some fantastic bluebell walks in the spring section of this book.

For summer, I chose some higher walks along the hilltops with magnificent, far-reaching views. Long summer days are the perfect time to visit the chalk grasslands, looking out for butterflies, wild flowers and scented herbs. The common spotted orchid thrives in the Chilterns, while the bright purple petals of the rare Chiltern gentian can be seen through August and September.

The beechwoods bring magnificent autumn colours, so the Ashridge Estate, Nettlebed and Burnham Beeches have all been selected for this season, but would equally make fantastic bluebell walks in spring.

In winter, the days are shorter and so are the walks. I have also chosen routes with firmer surfaces, that are not too far from a welcoming pub and village. Winter is a good time of year to spot birds of prey, including sparrowhawk, buzzards and kestrel, while the magnificent red kite now reigns supreme in the Chiltern skies, and can be admired at any time of year.

The distance and terrain are listed at the start of each walk, and as I always walk with my whippet, Albie, for company, I have also added details on the dog-friendliness of the walks, including where you might find livestock and stiles. I tried to keep road walking to a minimum, but where it is unavoidable, there are either pavements or wide verges to follow.

I know you will love this collection of walks just as much as I do. One of the pleasures of owning a dog is that you have to go out for a walk in all seasons, and this has shown me that the countryside has something magical to offer, all year round.

*Ruth Paley*

## PUBLISHER'S NOTE

We hope that you obtain considerable enjoyment from this book; great care has been taken in its preparation. Although at the time of publication all routes followed public rights of way or permitted paths, diversion orders can be made and permissions withdrawn.

We cannot, of course, be held responsible for such diversion orders and any inaccuracies in the text which result from these or any other changes to the routes, nor any damage which might result from walkers trespassing on private property. We are anxious though that all the details covering the walks are kept up to date and would therefore welcome information from readers which would be relevant to future editions.

The simple sketched maps that accompany the walks in this book are based on notes made by the author whilst surveying the routes on the ground. They are designed to show you how to reach the start and to point out the main features of the overall circuit, and they contain a progression of numbers that relate to the paragraphs of the text.

However, for the benefit of a proper map, we do recommend that you purchase the relevant Ordnance Survey sheet covering your walk. Ordnance Survey maps are widely available, especially through booksellers and local newsagents.

*The flower-rich chalk grassland of Aston Rowant Nature Reserve supports 30 different species of butterfly.*

spring

# 1 Cowleaze Wood and Aston Rowant Nature Reserve

### 3 miles / 4.8km

Cowleaze Wood is beautiful all year round, but from late April to May the woodland floor is carpeted with bluebells and it is a truly magical spot to explore. There are plenty of easy-to-follow paths through the wood and it's a popular picnic spot with families in spring. Our walk starts at Cowleaze Wood, where you can explore the bluebells at your leisure, then heads off into the tranquil Aston Rowant National Nature Reserve. With its chalk grassland perfect for wild flowers and insects, ancient beach woodland, wild juniper and hawthorn scrub, the nature reserve is a blissful spot on a spring day. As you admire the panoramic view across the north-western scarp of the Chilterns, you are also sure to spot red kites soaring above the hills. Natural England manages the landscape by the traditional method of grazing livestock, in order to control the spread of young scrub and create space for

# THE CHILTERNS  Year Round Walks

## The Facts

**Terrain** There are some gentle up and downhill sections, with one stretch at point 6 which might get you out of breath, but it's only for about 100 metres. The ground is firm underfoot so shouldn't get too muddy. There is a short stretch at the start of the bridleway, the rest of the walk follows public footpaths over grassy ground.

**Map** OS Explorer 171 Chiltern Hills West.

**Starting point** The information board at the free car park at Cowleaze Wood. (GR SU 726959).

**How to get there & parking** Cowleaze Wood is halfway between Lewknor and Stokenchurch, and just south of the M40 at junction 5. Heading from the north, just after you pass Hill Road, look out for the turning into the car park on the left. As the car park runs parallel with the road, you can see the cars before you spot the turning. The Sat nav postcode takes you to the road, then keep driving for a few minutes to find the turning for the car park. **Sat nav:** HP14 3YL.

**Refreshments** There is a large grassy picnic area next to the car park often with an ice cream van, but bring a picnic blanket as, strangely, it only has one bench. You pass picnic tables between points 1 and 2, as well as benches strategically placed for great views. The highly recommended Fox and Hounds is in nearby Christmas Common (topfoxpub.co.uk) and in Lewknor there's the dog-friendly Leathern Bottle (theleathernbottle.co.uk).

wild flowers to flourish. This important work is carried out by a dedicated team of around 300 speckle-faced Beulah sheep, and where you are likely to find them is noted in the walking instructions, in case you have a canine companion. On a spring day, listen out for the distinctive drumming of the woodpecker searching for a mate in the woodland. As well as the bluebells in Cowleaze, spring also brings the lovely white blossom of whitebeam, which fills the hedgerows with a wonderful scent. Painted white arrows along the route help keep you on track on this easy-to-navigate walk.

## The Walk

❶ Cross the road by the information board and you find yourself next to a bridleway sign. Turn right here and follow the path as it runs parallel with the

# Cowleaze Wood & Aston Rowant Nature Reserve

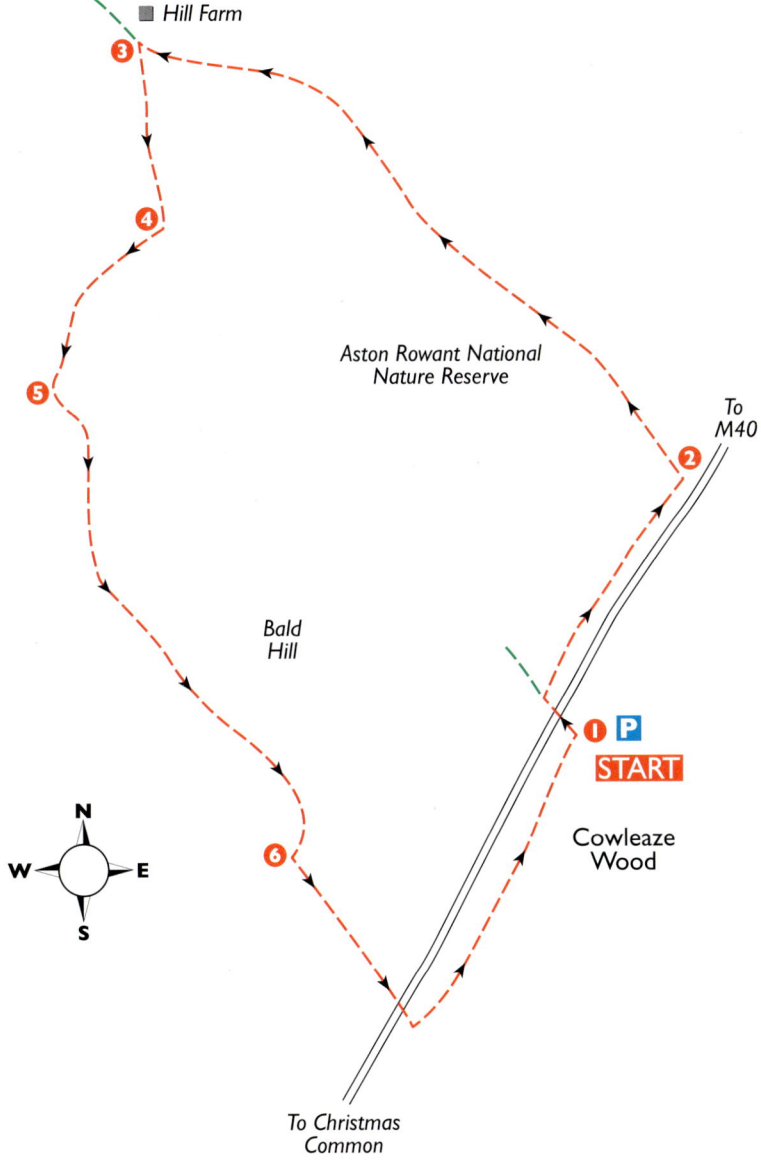

road for about 200m. You can see (and hear) the M40 in front of you, and the impressive hill beyond is **Beacon Hill**. Look out for a metal farm gate with a wooden gate next to it on your left, go through the gate to follow the public footpath.

# THE CHILTERNS  Year Round Walks

*Cowleaze Wood is carpeted with bluebells in late April and May.*

❷ Walk ahead, admiring the view in front of you across **Aston Rowant Nature Reserve**. Go through a metal gate and continue ahead, then through another gate into a large field sloping down towards **Hill Farm** – if you have a dog, keep an eye out for sheep here. There is a large map at the bottom of the field. Go through the wooden gate.

❸ Now you will see a choice of paths. We want the rutted path on the left which leads uphill past an '**Unsuitable for motor vehicles**' sign. The hedgerows here are filled with blossom in springtime.

❹ When you get to an information board and map, turn right and walk by the side of the wooden gate, looking out for the witch's broom tree by the path. The ground slopes away on your right and we are now in the heart of the nature reserve – this is my favourite part of the walk.

# Cowleaze Wood & Aston Rowant Nature Reserve

**5** Eventually, you come to a wooden gate leading to large fields where there are often sheep. Go through the gate then turn left and follow the fence uphill. Go through a gate, passing a **Natural England sign**, and continue ahead keeping the fence on your left. When you reach the end of the field, the path veers right. Finally you come to a wooden farm gate on your left with a white arrow painted on it.

**6** Go through the gate and follow the path steeply uphill with hawthorn bushes either side. When you get to the top, go through a metal gate with another white arrow – look out for sheep here. Cross the field straight ahead to another gate with a sign marked '**Lewknor 1½**'. Then cross the road and follow the path left back to the car park.

## What to look out for –

There is a wonderful example of a tree decorated with witch's broom just after you go through the gate at point 4, the large twiggy balls make it impossible to miss. They are caused by a deformity or fungus, which creates a dense mass of shoots all growing from a single point. Witch's broom is the perfect B&B for moths, who use them for food and shelter for their larvae.

The grassland provides an ideal habitat for butterflies, with some 30 species recorded on the reserve, including chalkhill blue, the black and white grizzled skipper and the small, brown dingy skipper.

*spring*

*Rothschild canal bridge over the Wendover Arm of the Grand Union Canal.*

# 2 Wendover Canal and Woods

### 7 miles / 11.2km

**T**his wonderful walk starts at the clock tower in the heart of historic Wendover, then follows a peaceful stretch by the Grand Union Canal, with far-reaching views across the rolling countryside. Leave the canal for a walk through Wendover Woods, the highest point in the Chilterns, and pass the popular Café in the Woods – with plenty of picnic tables to tempt weary walkers. You also pass literally under GoApe, so don't be surprised if someone suddenly swings into a giant rope net or hurtles over your head on a zip wire. Wendover Woods cover 800 acres of rich and varied habitat, and the bluebells in spring are spectacular. Return from the woods to enjoy the many charms of Wendover, and a well deserved rest in one of its many excellent pubs or cafés.

## Wendover Canal and Woods

### The Facts

**Terrain** Level path by the canal then uphill into Wendover Woods. Short steep downward section out of the wood, then roadside and pavements back into Wendover. The walk is firm underground and recommended for all seasons.

**Map** OS Explorer 181 Chiltern Hills North.

**Starting point** Wendover clock tower. (GR SP 869078).

**How to get there & parking** Wendover is five miles south-east of Aylesbury, off the A413. Head for the town centre, there's roadside parking on Wharf Road, or a library car park that's free on Sundays. **Sat nav: HP22 6EG.**

**Refreshments** Café in the Woods is a great place to stop and rest your legs (cafeinthewoods.co.uk). There are also plenty of excellent pubs and cafés in Wendover. The Red Lion on the High Street (redlionhotelwendover.co.uk) has lots of character with a small, shady seating area at the back.

## The Walk

❶ From the clock tower walk down **Aylesbury Road**, passing the **George and Dragon** on your right. Turn right down **Wharf Road** where you can get your first glimpse of **Wendover Woods**. The turning for the canal is just after the school patrol sign on your left, if you get to the school you've missed it!

❷ Walk along the towpath with the canal on your right. This part of the canal can be overgrown in places and is no longer accessible for boats, but it's the perfect habitat for ducks and you soon leave the houses behind to walk with a lovely view across the fields. Look out to your left for the monument on top of **Coombe Hill** when you get to No. 10 bridge (known locally as Perch Bridge).

❸ When you come to No. 9 bridge, the path takes you up to **Halton** village. Cross the road to a map and information board, then continue along the towpath, passing another information board and under a bridge with attractive blue ironwork.

❹ About 20m before a brick arched bridge, take a footpath on your right that leads you away from the canal. Don't follow it all the way up to the road, instead turn right again, following the public footpath sign and passing a **MOD sign** on your right. Walk through mixed woodland until you come to a public

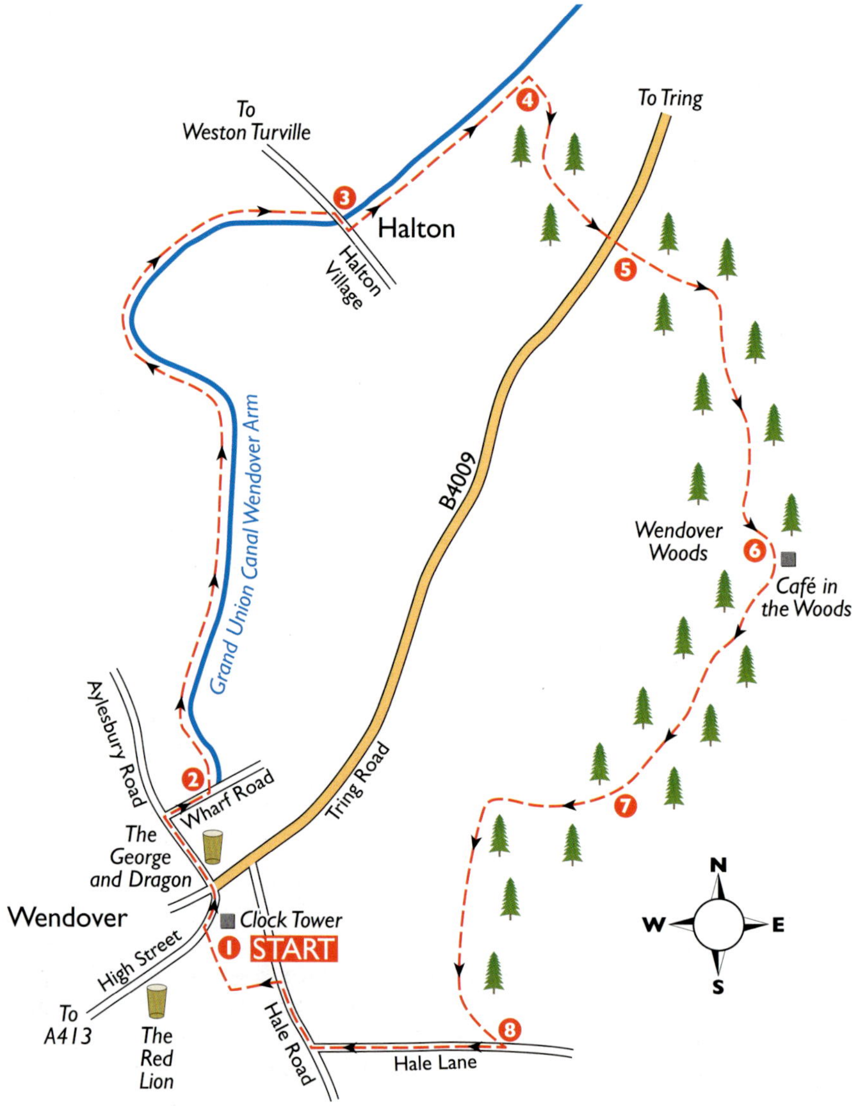

# THE CHILTERNS  Year Round Walks

*spring*

footpath with a car park down on your left. Turn right here and walk slightly uphill, passing yew trees, then through some metal bollards to a road. Turn left, then left again, following a public footpath on a shady path through more yew trees and heading slightly uphill. The path leads you through green bollards to another road where you turn left. Now walk roadside, passing **Rosemead** on your left.

14

# Wendover Canal and Woods  2

*Wendover Woods offer bluebells in spring and stunning colour in autumn.*

**5** You come to a road that you cross, then walk up **Mansion Hill**, passing a public footpath sign on your left, and into **Wendover Woods**. The path leads uphill. Ignore a cross path after about 100m, and follow the main sunken path past ancient yew trees. Keep on this path, passing a sign to the car park, and the spotters trail, then, at the road, turn right to the car park, café and GoApe.

**6** Pass the café and GoApe on your left, then pass two No Entry signs and keep going, under a zip wire, until you come to a large BBQ area ahead of you. Turn left, walking past an overflow parking area, with a picnic area on your right. Keep in this direction, as the path begins to lead downhill. Pass a sign for **Wendover Woods Fitness Trail**, then come to the northern entrance of the Iron Age **Boddington Camp** hillfort.

# THE CHILTERNS  Year Round Walks

**7** Take the path to the right of the sign and about 100m on your right, take the public footpath sign that leads you steeply downhill. This path is known as 'the snakey' and it's easy to see why. When you come to a wide footpath, turn left for an easy stretch of path, with good views to your right across the **Vale of Aylesbury**. When you come to a large open area, turn sharp right down to the road and out of Wendover Woods.

**8** Turn right to follow **Hale Lane** to a signpost. Turn right, following the sign for **'Village Centre'**. When you come to a sign for **Bridleway/Wendover Station**, follow the footpath until you come to a stream. Now turn right, following the **Ridgeway** sign along **Heron Path** until you find yourself once more by the clock tower.

*spring*

## What to look out for –

The overgrown **Wendover Arm** is no good for boats, but perfect for wildlife. There are always waterbirds to spot here and, if you are very lucky, you might also spot a kingfisher. These brightly coloured birds feed on aquatic insects, including dragonfly larvae and water beetles, as well as small fish. In spring, kingfishers elaborately court each other by the male offering the female a fish. He will attempt to feed the fish to the female, and if unsuccessful, can then console himself by eating the fish. They make tunnels in the bank to a nesting chamber where the female lays her eggs. Kingfishers are not endangered, although they are very sensitive to the cold, and harsh winters can cause their numbers to plummet drastically.

*Picturesque Bradenham Village Green is fringed with 18th-century brick and flint cottages.*

# 3 Bradenham Estate

**3 miles / 4.8km**

This walk explores the beech woodland and rolling valleys of the Bradenham Estate. This ancient woodland is carpeted with bluebells in spring, while the fields are fringed with wide hedgerows and flower margins. Starting in the delightful village of Bradenham, which is managed by the National Trust, take time to admire the red brick 17th-century manor house which sits at the top of a triangular green, dotted with brick and flint cottages. There are a few benches around the green and it's the perfect spot for a picnic, while watching the cricket in the summer, and looking out over the Chiltern hills. The origins of the village name Bradenham date back to Anglo-Saxon times, and mean 'broad enclosure'. Sitting on the green, looking out on the surrounding beech-topped hills, you can clearly see that the village does indeed sit in a broad valley. A former tenant of the manor house was Isaac D'Israeli, father of the Victorian Prime Minister, Benjamin Disraeli. Benjamin loved this area and bought Hughenden Manor, a few miles east of here. This house is now also owned by the National Trust and is open to visitors.

# THE CHILTERNS Year Round Walks

**Terrain** Woodland and field paths. Some uphill sections but nothing too strenuous. No road walking or stiles and dog friendly.

**Map** OS Explorer 172 Chiltern Hills East.

**Starting point** The free National Trust car park in the eastern corner of the village green. (GR SU 827970).

**How to get there & parking** Bradenham is four miles north-west of High Wycombe. Heading north along the A4010, the village is a right turn. At the village green, turn right, then first left up a bumpy track to the parking area. Sat nav: HP14 4HF.

**Refreshments** The Red Lion Bradenham is on the corner of Bradenham Wood Lane, as you turn off the A4010. This friendly, licensed café welcomes walkers and serves food from breakfast time onwards. It doesn't have a website but you can look at TripAdvisor for reviews and photos.

## The Walk

**1** Follow the path behind the car park, heading away from the village and the green, with the brick walls of **Bradenham Manor** garden on your left. The track turns left to follow the wall uphill, passing a '**No Unauthorised Vehicles**' sign. The path then turns left, but you need to take the public bridleway into the woods, soon heading uphill. Stay on this path, ignoring any side turns. When

*Stopping to admire the view towards Bradenham Beeches at Point 3.*

## Bradenham Estate    3

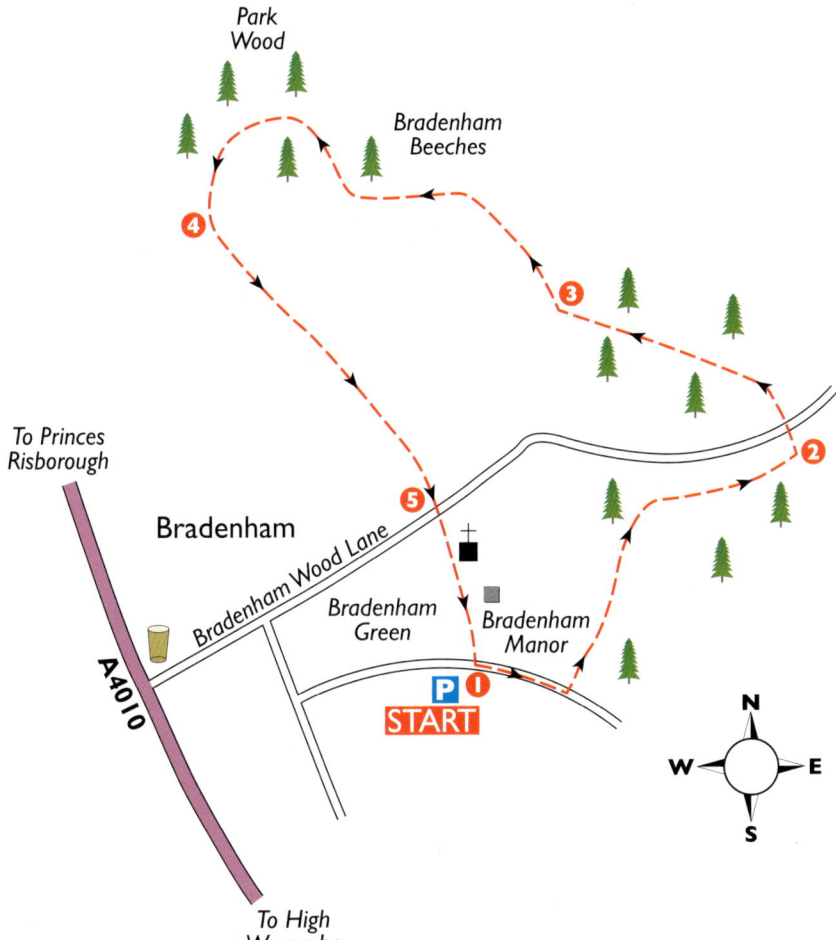

you come to a fork, turn left and you will find yourself walking parallel with the road below you. Follow the path and shortly you come to a cross path – turn left again to follow the path down to the road.

**2** There is a public footpath sign by the road, cross with care and follow the path directly ahead of you back into woods, passing a **National Trust** horseshoe sign on your right. Stay on this path, looking out for the odd horseshoe sign, with a chain link fence on your right. When this fence curves away to the right, take the path downhill. There is a gate into a field on your left here, don't go through the gate, instead turn right and head steeply downhill along a narrow path to some gates on your left and a stunning view across the **Bradenham Valley**.

# THE CHILTERNS  Year Round Walks

❸ Take the gate on the right that leads into a meadow, with a bench if you want to stop and admire the view. Follow the path diagonally across the field to a track, with gates about 20m away on your right. Cross the track and follow the path steeply up a short hill to a bench. Pass the bench and go through the swing gate into **Bradenham Beeches**, following the public footpath. Keep an eye out for the horseshoe signs and turn left at a junction, heading downhill. At a 'V' junction, again take the path on your left.

❹ The path leads you out of the woods. Turn left, and walk by the field edge back towards **Bradenham**. Cross a track and continue straight on, with the woods now up on your left.

❺ Go through two gates to walk by the side of the **Old School House** to the road. Cross with care, then pass **St Botolph Church** and the **Manor House** to return to the car park.

## What to look out for –

In spring, before the trees come out in full leaf, the woodland floor is carpeted with bluebells. The bluebell has adapted to woodland life by completing its life cycle while light levels are high, with the bulbs ensuring that they have the energy store to quickly grow each spring.

**Bradenham Wood** is a **Site of Special Scientific Interest**, with some 28 species of butterfly recorded in the area. The best time for butterfly spotting is a warm, dry day between April and September. It's also a good spot for hearing the distinctive song of the skylark, as you return to Bradenham across the fields.

*spring*

*Passing a traditional Chiltern brick and flint cottage.*

*spring*

# *4* Hughenden Valley

### 4.5 miles / 7.2km

The Hughenden Valley has been cut deeply into the chalk hills, and at its base runs a small chalk stream, its size very much depending on recent rainfall. This walk offers stunning views across the valley as you walk through the airy beechwood at Millfield Wood nature reserve. The wood dates back to medieval times, and this habitat supports many beautiful Chiltern flowers typical of ancient woodland, including wood anemone, yellow archangel, wood sorrel and coralroot, which flowers in April and May. The trees are home to woodpeckers, whose distinctive tapping on the tree trunks is clearly heard on spring days as they mark their territory. At Cryers Hill you could take a break at the friendly White Lion pub, before returning across meadows to the final stretch of the walk by the chalk stream and the panoramic National Trust parkland of Hughenden, former home of the charismatic Victorian Prime Minister, Benjamin Disraeli.

## The Walk

**1** Follow the pavement up Hughenden Road, with the park on your left. After about 150m, before you get to the buildings ahead, look out for a narrow gap in the hedgerow that leads you up to **Hughenden Road**. You will be right by the 40mph road signs, cross the road with care and walk up the steps to the public footpath opposite. Go through the kissing gate then walk uphill, with the field on your left.

# CHILTERNS Year Round Walks

**Terrain** There are a few uphill sections and stiles, as this walk crosses fields and takes you through woodland, with some roots growing over the path.

**Map** OS Explorer 172 Chiltern Hills East.

**Starting point** The small car park by the side of Hughenden Road. (GR SU 865946).

**How to get there & parking** From the centre of High Wycombe, follow the Hughenden Road/A4128, signed, following the brown signs for Hughenden Manor and heading north out of the town. Look out for the parking spot on your left, just past the 30mph sign and at the point where the houses stop. **Sat nav:** HP13 5PE.

**Refreshments** The White Lion (☎ 01494 713900) at Cryers Hill is a traditional pub and open from 11.30am to 11pm. It serves food and has a large inglenook fireplace and picnic tables outside. Towards the end of the walk you cross the parkland of the National Trust property Hughenden Manor, and a short detour takes you to the delightful Stableyard Café, serving hot and cold lunches, cakes and drinks (nationaltrust.org.uk/hughenden). Dogs are welcome in the outside seating area.

*Exploring the lush meadows in the Hughenden Estate.*

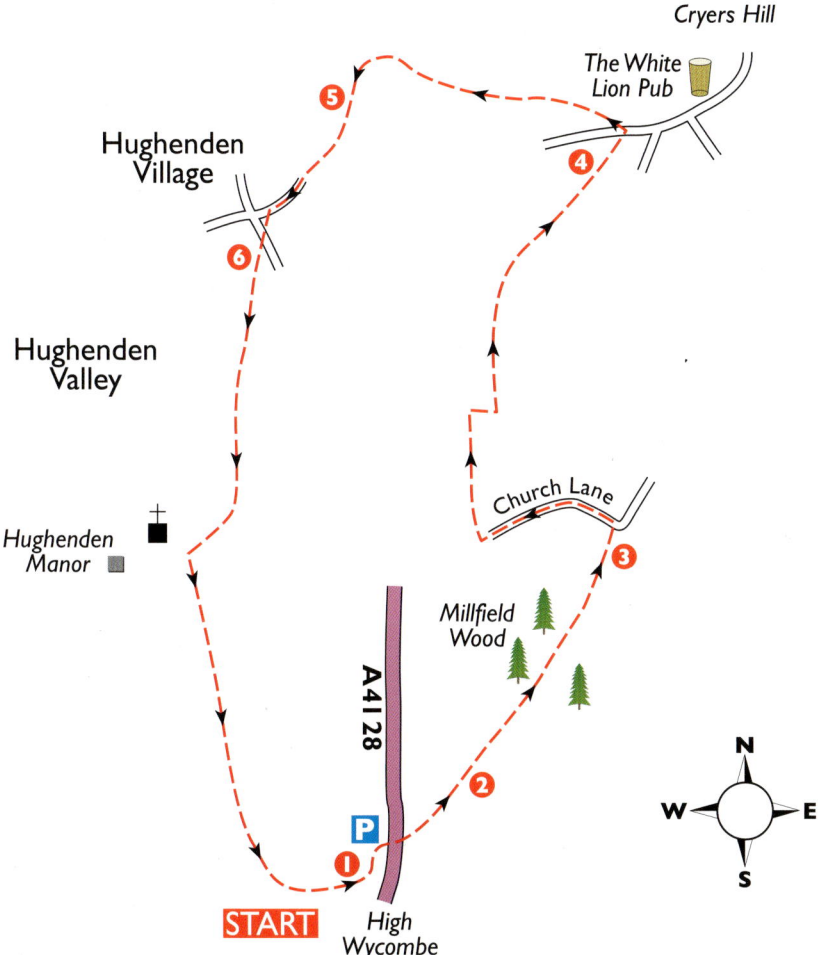

# Hughenden Valley

❷ Go through a gate at the top of the field, then walk a few metres to a cross-path. Turn left and follow the shady path gently uphill, with glimpses of the valley through the trees on your left. Go through a metal gate and continue ahead, then through another gate into **Millfield Wood** nature reserve. Follow the path through the wood, ignoring side paths and passing an information board on your left. Cross a stile out of the wood, then walk diagonally right across a field (there are often horses here but they are very used to walkers) to another stile.

❸ Turn left down **Church Lane**, heading roughly west until you come to a

# CHILTERNS  Year Round Walks

footpath sign on your right. Follow this path, heading north until you get to **Cryers Hill Road**.

④ If you want to detour to the White Lion, follow the road right. Otherwise cross the road and follow the public footpath along a surfaced drive. Bear left after about 50m, and continue until you come to the 'Moggie Hotel', where you cross a stile to follow the public footpath to the right. Follow the narrow path down to a kissing gate and cross path, admiring the views to the left as you walk.

⑤ Turn left and follow the drive past some delightful cottages. The drive becomes **Boss Lane** and leads you down to the main road in Hughenden Village, just by the roundabout. Turn left and walk down **Valley Road** for about 20m. Cross the road and take the signed footpath by the bus stop that leads you up a few steps then turns left, right in front of the Village Store.

⑥ This path leads you to the drive of **Hughenden Park**, by the church. Following the drive to your right takes you to the house, gardens and café, but to continue the walk carry on ahead across the parkland, soon walking with the stream on your left. Cross the bridge and head back to the car park.

## What to look out for –

Disraeli's legendary flattery even charmed Queen Victoria and evidence of her affection for him is on display in **Hughenden Manor**, where she gifted him a portrait of herself. Victoria visited the Manor in 1877, and Disraeli carefully arranged for the legs of one of the dining chairs to be reduced in height to avoid the embarrassment of her royal legs not touching the floor.

In more recent history, Hughenden Manor was the base for a secret map-making organisation during the Second World War and you can explore the atmospheric cellars and ice house where this period of history has been carefully recreated. There is also an annual 1940s weekend in September (nationaltrust.org.uk/hughenden).

*Heading south across Drunken Bottom.*

# 5 Hailey and Ipsden
### 3.5 miles / 5.6km

Exploring a remote corner of south Oxfordshire, this walk starts in the sleepy hamlet of Hailey, then heads north to Wicks Wood, filled with birdsong and flowers in spring. Follow the Chiltern Way, to cross fields buzzing with bumblebees and butterflies, passing Drunken Bottom and Coblers Hill, where there are wonderful, wide, expansive views across the Chiltern landscape. As you skirt the edge of Ipsden, pause to admire its Celtic-style war memorial, before heading back along quiet country lanes to the King William IV pub. This lovely inn welcomes walkers and the picnic tables outside offer fantastic views across the Chiltern hills. As well as lots of red kites, you might also spot cyclists on this route as part of it follows the Chiltern Cycleway, and if you fancied a different option, the whole walk could easily be done by mountain bike.

## The Walk

**1** With your back to the pub, turn right and walk down the narrow lane. At the footpath sign '**Chiltern Way extension**' on your right, turn and follow the

# THE CHILTERNS  Year Round Walks

**Terrain**  Half on surfaced paths, and half across fields, this is a good route after rainy weather. It's also mainly level, with views of hills rather than actually walking up and down them. There are no stiles and very little traffic, as any roads passed are 'Quiet Lanes'.

**Map**  OS Explorer 171 Chiltern Hills West.

**Starting point**  The King William IV pub. (GR SU 642858).

**How to get there & parking**  The village of Hailey is a few miles south of the A4130 and the pub is on the far eastern edge of the village, past the church. The pub has a sign welcoming walkers in the overflow car park – but check with the landlord first and if you are parking in a pub car park, as a courtesy it's best to stop for a drink! **Sat nav:** OX10 6AD.

**Refreshments**  The King William IV has plenty of tables outside with stunning views across this unspoilt part of south Oxfordshire, and there's a log fire inside this cosy country pub for colder days. Dogs are also welcome (kingwilliamhailey.co.uk).

*A kite soars over the fields by the stone bench at point 4.*

## Hailey and Ipsden    5

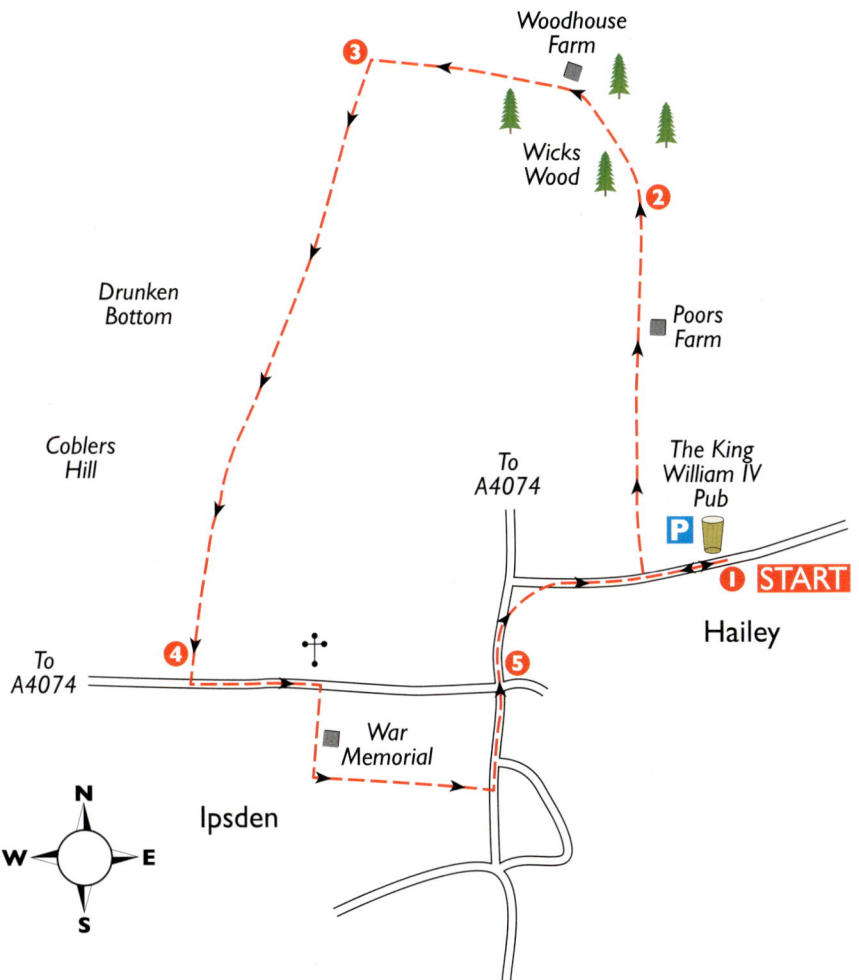

*spring*

path. The path passes **Poors Farm** and there are good views over to your left of the remaining cooling towers at **Didcot Power Station**. Continue straight ahead, ignoring a turn to your right, and follow the footpath straight across the field to **Wicks Wood**.

**②** Now follow the **Chiltern footpath** sign straight into the wood. Walk ahead then at the junction turn left, then straight on, following the **Chiltern Way**. Eventually, the path leads downhill and you leave these lovely woods to find yourself in front of **Woodhouse Farm**. Turn left and follow the Chiltern Way to a junction, where you turn left, passing some houses on your left.

27

# THE CHILTERNS  Year Round Walks

*spring*

❸ Cross the road and take the bridleway, as it leads you slightly uphill towards **Drunken Bottom**. The path levels off and you walk across a beautiful arable landscape, filled with butterflies and birdsong. Towards the end of this path, you will spot **St Mary the Virgin church**, in **Ipsden**, on your left.

❹ When you get to the road, turn left and walk into Ipsden. Opposite the church, turn right and follow the bridleway, passing the war memorial. There are a few benches along this stretch if you want to stop for a while and watch the kites. At the end of the field, by a stone bench, turn left and follow a narrow footpath through trees until you come to a road and some houses.

❺ Turn left and walk up the road, passing **Crabtree Corner**. At the crossroads go straight on, following the sign '**Hailey via Quiet Lane**'. A footpath sign directs you across the corner of the field, then turn right, following the edge of the field back to the pub.

## What to look out for –

The distinctive **Ipsden War Memorial** commemorates residents killed or missing during the First and Second World Wars and, unusually, stands alone by the side of a field, rather than being in the centre of the hamlet.

There are bluebells in **Wicks Wood** and spring flowers to admire on this walk, while the fields hum with the sound of bumblebees and butterflies from late spring onwards.

28

*Taking time to admire the view from the stone topograph above Princes Risborough.*

# 6 Princes Risborough and Whiteleaf Cross

### 7 miles / 11.2km

Princes Risborough, with its shops and cafés, is a useful starting point for a splendid walk that leads you across the heart of the Chiltern landscape, enjoying sweeping views and the chalk hill figure of the Whiteleaf Cross. This interesting feature is on Whiteleaf Hill, along with a burial mound and First World War practice trenches. The cross has dominated the landscape for centuries, although its history is unknown. You also pass two characterful pubs, England's oldest smock mill and beautiful beech woodland, before arriving on top of Brush Hill Local Nature Reserve, with a panoramic view across the valley.

# THE CHILTERNS  Year Round Walks

**Terrain** There are up and downhill sections to this walk, but you will be rewarded by fantastic views. A series of wooden steps at the end of the walk leads you back into town. There are stiles across some of the fields which can have cattle in them, with muddy patches by the gates. I did this walk with a medium-sized dog who managed to get through all the stiles. You pass through paddocks in the middle of the walk so dogs need to be on leads there. There is a short amount of road walking along quiet lanes.

**Map** OS Explorer 181 Chiltern Hills North.

**Starting point** Horns Lane Pay and Display car park. (GR SP 809033).

**How to get there & parking** Princes Risborough is halfway between Thame and Great Missenden. The A4010 runs through the town and the various car parks are all clearly signed. The entrance to the Horns Lane car park is on New Road, as you head out of town towards Great Hampden. The car park has toilets and is free on Sundays and Bank Holidays.
**Sat nav:** HP27 0AW.

**Refreshments** You pass two excellent pubs as you walk, both serve food, are open every day and well worth spending time in: the Whip Inn (thewhipinn.co.uk) and Pink & Lily (pink-lily.com).

## The Walk

**1** From the car park, turn left and walk into the town centre, down **Bell Street** and passing the library then the **Bell** pub on the other side of the street. By a pedestrian crossing, take the signed footpath on the left and walk up the surfaced path. Go through the metal barriers to a road, then turn left and walk uphill, over **Merton Road** to a field.

**2** Turn left and follow the footpath skirting the edge of the field, cross the **Ridgeway** path, and continue ahead in the same direction, by a large arable field. The path goes down, then uphill – look out for **Whiteleaf Cross** on your left. At the end of the field, go through a gap in the hedge and straight on across the next field. Cross two stiles and continue in the same direction, following the **Chiltern Society footpath**. The impressive house on your left is the early 19th-century Wardrobes. Cross its drive and continue ahead for a short distance, before crossing a stile in the hedge on your left. Cross another stile then walk ahead to the road.

## Princes Risborough and Whiteleaf Cross    6

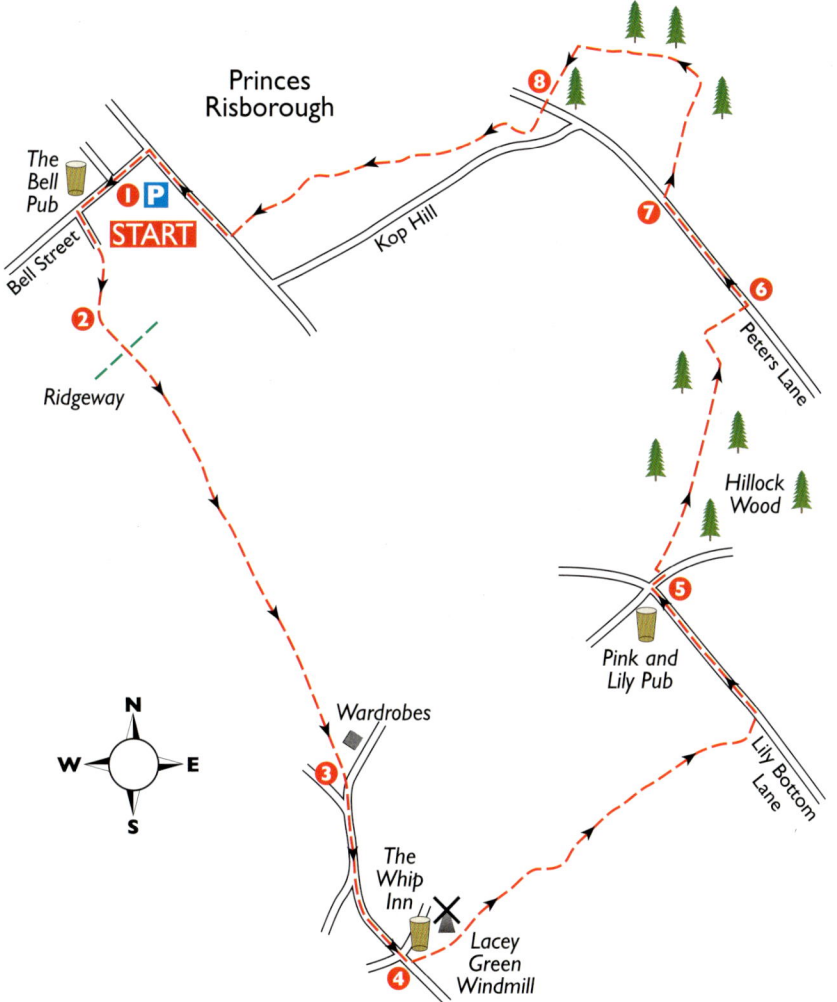

③ You are now at a T-junction on the edge of **Loosely Row**. Cross the road and walk up **Woodway** into the village. There is no pavement initially, but the verge is wide enough to walk on with ease as you admire the classic Chiltern flint and brick cottages. Pass the **Whip Inn** and a path leading to the **Lacey Green Windmill**, then walk about 10m down **Pink Road** to a swing gate and the **Chiltern Way** footpath, just before the elaborate bus shelter.

④ Go through the gate and ahead, admiring the windmill as you pass. You now need to stay on the Chiltern Way, crossing diagonally across a paddock,

# THE CHILTERNS  Year Round Walks

*summer*

*The age and purpose of the Whiteleaf Cross remains a mystery to this day.*

over a stile and turning left along a path between paddocks. Go through a gate then turn left on the surfaced **Lily Bottom Lane**, that leads you to **Parslow's Hillock** and the **Pink and Lily** pub.

**5** Turn right along the verge for a few metres, then cross to a surfaced track to the left of **Woodlands**. Follow the track round to the right and through a gate to a bridleway. Now stay on this track through the woods until you come to a field. Turn right and follow the path by the side of the field to the road.

**6** Turn left and walk along the road, passing a series of cottages. Just past the last cottage, '**Hailey**', turn right to follow the bridleway.

**7** Cross a field to a gate on the other side, straight across a bridleway and pass a gate into woods. Now stay on the bridleway, skirting the edge of the wood for 200m until you come to a junction. Keep left and follow the bridleway for 750m until you come to a track and the **Ridgeway**. It's worth a quick diversion here to view the ancient **Whiteleaf Cross** up on your right. Then turn left past the First World War trenches to get to the busy **Whiteleaf Hill car park**.

## Princes Risborough and Whiteleaf Cross

**8** Cross the road and go through the gate on the other side. A path leads left through **Brush Hill Local Nature Reserve** until you can shortly see a stone topograph through the fence. Go through the gate to take in the magnificent panoramic view before you. Then follow the path in front of the stone, which leads you downhill. A few steps take you to a gate, then down more steps. When you come to a sign for the Ridgeway, turn left for a short distance and when you get to the road, turn right to return to the car park.

### What to look out for –

The **Lacey Green Windmill** still has its unique wooden machinery, dating back to around 1650, making this the oldest smock windmill in the country. Smock mills are named after their resemblance to the smocks once traditionally worn by farmers. Its working life ended in 1915, after which the wooden structure rapidly deteriorated. But it is once more in pristine condition, having been lovingly restored back to working order by The Chiltern Society. Their website has photos of what it looked like before the restoration, as well as opening times if you want to visit (laceygreenwindmill.org.uk).

*The hanger of mature beech once provided timber for High Wycombe's chairmakers. Local 'bodgers' made their living by crafting the turned legs for chairs.*

*summer*

# 7 Radnage to Lodge Hill

### 4.5 miles / 7.2km

On a summer's day there's no better place than high on the Chiltern hills, admiring the view with a slight breeze to cool you down. This walk mainly follows field paths across chalk grassland, with a shady section through beech woodland at Yoesden nature reserve. The walk starts by the charming St Mary's church in Radnage, built by the Knights Templar in the late 12th or early 13th century, which has been used as a filming location for BBC TV's *Cranford* series. There are some steeper sections to this walk, but at the top of Lodge Hill are some benches with wonderful views where you can have a picnic and catch your breath, while towards the end of the walk, the Boot's beer garden is a perfect spot for a refreshment break. This is also a great walk for dog owners as almost the entire walk could be off lead by the side of large arable fields, with just one field towards the end with sheep, but this is clearly signed in advance.

## Radnage to Lodge Hill

### The Facts

**Terrain** Mainly field paths with some woodland in the middle of the walk. There is only 10 minutes of road walking, which is at the start of the walk, and no pavements, but it is a very quiet road. A few stiles and some short but steep up and downhill walking. There are some nettles by narrow footpaths so, in summer, long trousers might be a better option than shorts!

**Map** OS Explorer 171 Chiltern Hills West.

**Starting point** St Mary's church in Radnage. (GR SU 785979).

**How to get there & parking** Radnage is about seven miles north-west of High Wycombe. Take the A40 through West Wycombe, then take a right turn onto Chorley Road, then left onto Bottom Road which leads into the village. The church is in the north of the village, so continue along Horseshoe Road to Church Lane. There is no car park in the village so park roadside with care, avoiding driveways. **Sat nav:** HP14 4DU.

**Refreshments** You pass the Boot (theboot-bledlowridge.co.uk) towards the end of the walk, or there's the Crown (crownradnage.co.uk) in Radnage – both are excellent choices.

## The Walk

❶ From the church, turn right along **Church Lane**, which shortly turns into **Radnage Lane**. Ignore the first footpath sign on your right, but just before a turning to a barn on your left, turn right up a narrow path that leads steeply up the hill. You will find yourself walking with trees on your right and fields on your left, with a wonderful view across the valley.

❷ Cross the road and walk up **Routs Green** opposite you. Stay on the lane as it veers to the right, passing **Routs Green Farm**. As you pass the last house, the surfaced lane changes to a bridleway. Continue ahead and through a wooden gate, then straight on along a narrow path, now heading downhill. Follow the bridleway between large arable fields with **Lodge Hill** ahead of you on the horizon.

❸ When you get to the edge of the woods, there is a wooden post with footpath arrows pointing in various directions – you will be returning to this point later in the walk. Now turn left and follow a shady path at the edge of the wood. Pass **Callow Down Farm** down on your left, and go through a metal

# THE CHILTERNS Year Round Walks

*summer*

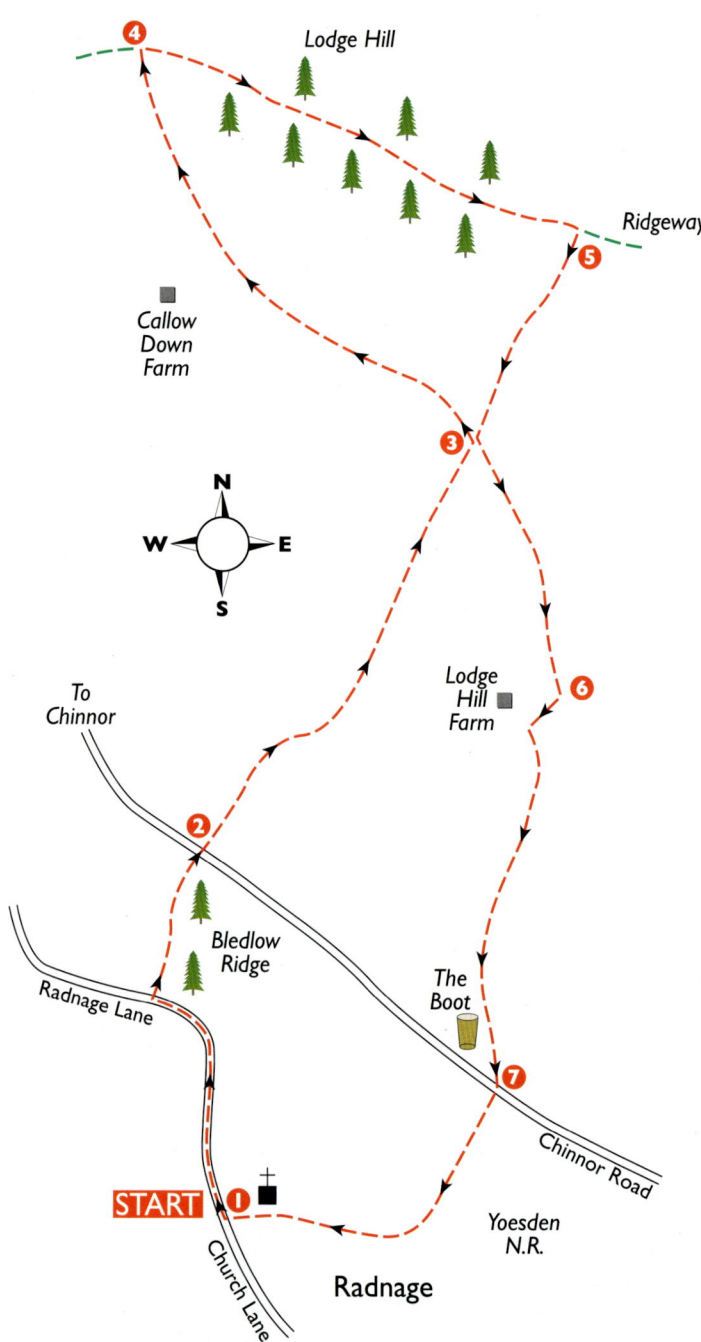

## Radnage to Lodge Hill   7

*Admiring the rolling landscape at point 6 of the walk.*

farm gate with a **'Circular Ride'** sign. Cross the next field and you come to the **Ridgeway**.

**4** Turn right and follow the well-trodden path up towards **Lodge Hill**. Now keep following the Ridgeway through woods until you reach the top of the hill, where you can catch your breath and admire the spectacular views from the top. Walk through a patch of ancient beech trees, passing another Ridgeway sign. At the Ridgway sign after this, turn right and cross the stile, leaving the Ridgeway which continues ahead.

**5** Walk down the hill – you can see the path you took to get here snaking across the fields ahead of you. Walk to the post at point 3, and then continue to the edge of the field. Now turn left and walk with the hedge on your right. The field leads you to a lane by **The Granary Barn**.

**6** Keep ahead until shortly you come to a **'Lodge Hill Farm'** sign where you turn right. Walk up to the farm buildings, then go through the kissing gate on your left and by the side of the field ahead. Look out for some conifers in

# THE CHILTERNS  Year Round Walks

the hedge on your right, and just next to them is a swing gate. Go through the gate and follow the public footpath up the field and through a metal swing gate, then veer to the left along the next field. Cross a stile and follow the path towards the road, which you can hear ahead of you.

**7** The **Boot** is just here on your right if you want a rest, otherwise cross the road and follow the public footpath sign directly opposite along a narrow path. There can be sheep and cows in the fields here, but all fenced off so don't worry if you have a dog with you. The path leads you into the delightful Yoesden Nature Reserve, with an information board on your left describing the wildlife. There are two footpaths just past the sign, take the one on the right then continue downhill, with views shortly opening up across **Bledlow Ridge**. Follow the path through gates and across a couple of fields until you come to a gate that leads to the back of **St Mary's churchyard**.

## What to look out for –

Listen out for the low thrum of insects in the wild-flower-rich habitat of **Yoesden nature reserve**. The steep slopes make this land inaccessible for ploughing. Instead, the grassland has been grazed by sheep since medieval times, controlling fast-growing grass and enabling a rich tapestry of wild flowers to thrive. Look out for pale yellow cowslips in spring, and pink and purple orchids in June. There are also wild herbs, including thyme and marjoram. The wild flowers in turn make this an important butterfly habitat, attracting four blues: small blue, chalkhill blue, Adonis blue and common blue.

*At 852 feet above sea level, Coombe Hill is the highest viewpoint in the Chilterns.*

# *8* Coombe Hill and Beacon Hill

### 7 miles / 11.2km

**If you only do one walk in the Chilterns,** make it this one! This fabulous walk starts in the picturesque market town of Wendover, with its attractive clock tower and welcoming pubs. You follow the Ridgeway through a nature reserve and up to Coombe Hill, the highest viewpoint in the Chilterns with sweeping views over the Aylesbury Vale. The monument on top is an iconic landmark that can often be spotted while walking in the Chilterns. It is dedicated to the men from Buckinghamshire who gave their lives during the Boer War and is a good spot to sit, watching the red kites soar in the skies around you. This chalk grassland is home to 30 species of wild flower and 28 species of butterfly. Cattle grazing the grassland over summer keep the grass short and allow wild flowers to thrive. The Ridgeway then dips down through majestic beechwoods for a shady stroll filled with birdsong. For the curious, this walk also offers a good view of the 16th-century manor house of Chequers – the official country residence of British Prime Ministers since 1921. You then walk round Beacon Hill, before heading back across fields to Wendover. This splendid walk is also very easy to navigate as it is almost entirely following either the Ridgeway or the Aylesbury Ring.

# THE CHILTERNS  Year Round Walks

**Terrain**  Grass tracks and woodland paths with a short stretch of road walking at the start. There are also up and downhill sections, although never too steep, with some steps and stiles.

**Map**  OS Explorer 181 Chiltern Hills North.

**Starting point**  The free car park by the cricket club off the Witchell in Wendover. (GR SP 868075).

**How to get there & parking**  Wendover is off the A413, halfway between Aylesbury and High Wycombe. From the High Street, turn down South Street and the Witchell is on the left, just past the King and Queen pub. Turn right off the Witchell into the small car park. **Sat nav:** HP22 6EG.

**Refreshments**  Wendover has plenty of good pubs, and this walk passes two of them at the start, the King and Queen and the Shoulder of Mutton. If you walk down the High Street you come to Rumsey's, a chocolatier with cakes and milkshakes that Willy Wonka himself would have been proud to serve – a popular choice with younger walkers! Halfway along the walk, you pass Buckmoorend Farm Shop which sells ice creams and has picnic tables where you can stop for a rest, and play with their very friendly sheepdog!

## The Walk

**1** From the **Witchell**, turn right along **South Street**, then left at the top of the road and cross the railway tracks. There is only a pavement on one side of the road, so you will need to cross the road, then as the road bends just before the 40mph signs, cross back with care where you see a small parking area and signs for the **Ridgeway**. Pass the information board and take the path on the right, through a metal gate, following the Ridgeway. This national trail is clearly signed with an acorn, so look out for the signs as you walk to make sure you are always on the right track.

**2** Walk up steps past trees and scrubland, and very soon you are rewarded with stunning views to the north. Go through a metal gate, passing another information board for **Bacombe Hill**, then continue ahead up to **Coombe Hill**. Cross a sunken path with gates on either side of it, then pass a sign for Coombe Hill and walk up to the monument.

**3** From the monument, follow the Ridgeway heading south. As you walk, you

## Coombe Hill and Beacon Hill

*Heading down to Ellesborough at point 7.*

can see **Coombe Hill Farm** down in the valley on your right, as well as the church in **Ellesborough**. The second half of this walk will take you past this church and across the fields back to **Wendover**. The Ridgeway takes you through a metal gate into beech woods. Walk through the woods until you come to the road.

**4** Turn right and walk for about 150m until you come to the drive of **Lodge Hill Game Farm** on the other side of the road. The Ridgeway path is right next to the drive. Follow the path through the woods, ignoring all side paths and keeping an eye out for the acorn Ridgeway signs. The path eventually leads to a road by **Buckmoorend Farm Shop**.

**5** Cross the road and go through the gate, following the Ridgeway path, with the private grounds of **Chequers** on your right. Cross the tree-lined drive of Chequers to follow the Ridgeway across fields, heading towards **Maple Wood** on the horizon. Go through a gate into the woods, then follow the path on your right, skirting the edge of the woods with Chequers still visible on your right. Go through a wooden gate and you see a wooden post.

**6** At this point you leave the Ridgeway to follow the public footpath by the side of **Whorley Wood**. Go through a kissing gate into the woods, then follow a path directly ahead of you, crossing a track marked '**Private**' on both sides. Stay on this footpath as it leads you through a gate and across a field to steps. You now pass through an ancient patch of boxwood, then out onto the slopes of **Beacon Hill**.

# THE CHILTERNS Year Round Walks

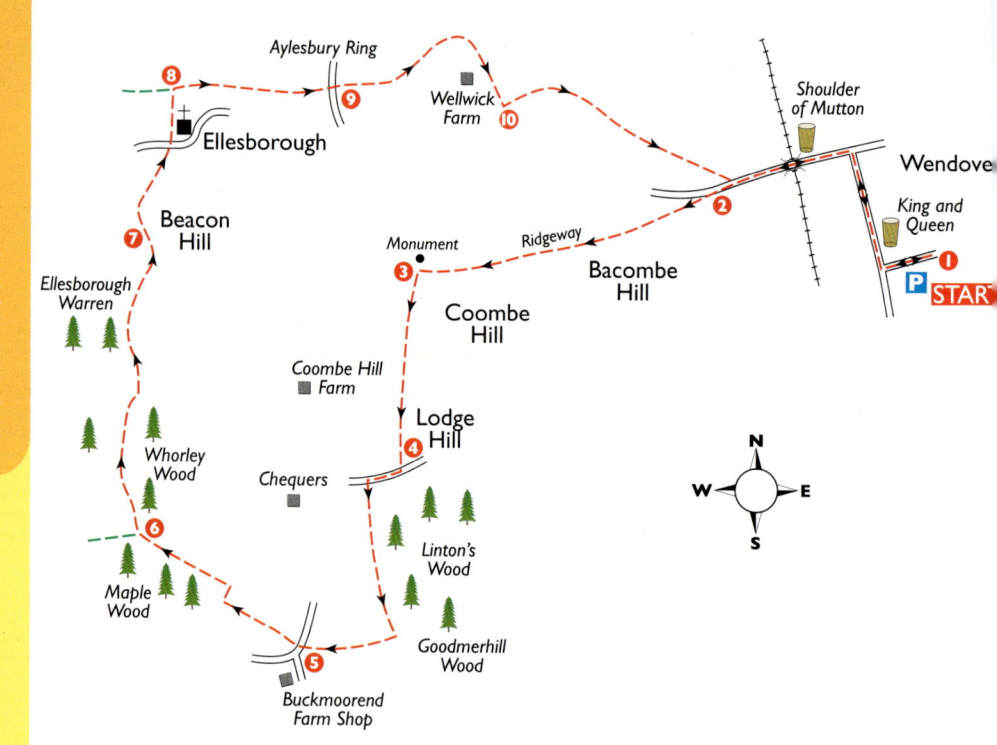

*summer*

⑦ The energetic could climb up to the top, otherwise follow the white chalk path across the hill to a swing gate, then walk across the field to **Ellesborough Manor**. Cross the road and follow the path by the left of the churchyard and down some steps. Go through a kissing gate then follow the footpath down the field.

⑧ Look out for the sign for the **Aylesbury Ring** (an Aylesbury duck on a white disk) and at the gate by a barbed wire fence, turn right and walk towards a brick building. Go through the kissing gate then follow the surfaced path past cottages. Pass **Springs Farm** on your left, and stay ahead on the footpath, ignoring the right turn which leads back into the village. Follow the path until you come to a road at the edge of **Butler's Cross**.

⑨ Turn left and follow the pavement for about 80m until you spot a metal farm gate on the other side of the road. Cross and follow the Aylesbury Ring across a series of arable fields, punctuated with stiles. When you reach the gates of **Wellwick Farm**, head straight on towards the house. Just before the entrance to the garden, cross the stile on your left. This leads you past the farm buildings

## Coombe Hill and Beacon Hill

to a drive. Stay on the Aylesbury Ring as it heads directly across the field ahead of you towards **Wendover**.

**10** When you reach a hedgerow with houses ahead, go through the swing gate to follow the path by the side of paddocks. Cross the last gate then follow the Aylesbury Ring path diagonally to the right across the field. The path leads you to the track, which in turn leads to **Ellesborough Road**. Turn left and retrace your steps back to the car.

## What to look out for –

Just before Beacon Hill, you pass through a stretch of ancient box woodland, with trees dating back to 1696. This is one of only three native box woodlands left in the country. Rare lichens and insects have established themselves here over the centuries, including large numbers of spiders! Box woodland was harvested for its timber, regarded by woodworkers as the best wood for engraving due to its high density. In the past, local lacemakers also used box to make bobbins, with Buckinghamshire being the centre of the English lacemaking industry during the 16th century. The steep sides of the slope have helped preserve this woodland, as it was too hard for farmers to use the land.

*Summer*

*The mineral rich River Chess is a chalk stream, with its water coming from the groundwater held in the chalk of the Chiltern Hills. It is ideal for growing watercress.*

# 9 Chenies and the Chess Valley

**6 miles / 9.6km**

This is a good choice for a sunny day, with shady stretches as you walk through woods and valleys, passing the 13th-century Chenies Manor House, once visited by Elizabeth I, before crossing the River Chess to explore Frogmore Meadow Nature Reserve and the Chess Valley. For the second stretch of the walk, enjoy stunning views across the rolling landscape before a lovely stretch by the banks of the river. Since the Middle Ages, the River Chess has played a significant role in the economy of the area, flooding the meadows and making the area perfect for watercress. Look out for trout, escaped from the Chess Valley Trout Farm, who have happily made these clear chalk waters their home.

## Chenies and the Chess Valley

### The Facts

**Terrain** Woods and field paths with no particularly steep sections. Good choice for dog walkers.

**Map** OS Explorer 172 Chiltern Hills East.

**Starting point** The small car park off Stony Lane. (GR TQ 005981).

**How to get there & parking** Chenies is to the east of Amersham and Little Chalfont, near the border with Hertfordshire. Stony Lane is off the A404 and runs north into Latimer. The small car park is on the left as you head north. **Sat nav:** HP6 6SP.

**Refreshments** You pass two pubs in Chenies – the Bedford Arms (bedfordarms.co.uk) and the Red Lion (theredlionchenies.co.uk).

## The Walk

**1** From the car park, cross the road and follow the public bridleway into **Walk Wood**. Soon the trees are replaced by stunning views to your left over the **Chiltern Hills**. The path ends with a house on your right. Continue ahead, through a wooden kissing gate, then follow the footpath back into woods. The path veers to the left and brings you to a cross track, where you continue straight on. Pass through a wooden barrier and continue following the path, following the **Heritage Trail**, with a fence on your left. You come to high brick walls, and continue ahead until you come to **St Michael's Church** and **Chenies Manor House**.

**2** Turn left and walk past the church following a gravel drive to the delightful village green, with its pump and bench if you want to stop for a break. Cross the green and follow the sign for **Chorleywood and Rickmansworth**, passing the **Bedford Arms** and the **Red Lion**. When you come to a red brick house with prominent chimneys, opposite **Chenies and Latimer Cricket Club**, turn left and through the gate to follow the **Chiltern Way**.

**3** Follow the narrow path, then through another gate into woods. Stay on the Chiltern Way to cross a field. Turn left at the end of the field, following the arrow, then a right turn into woods. Go through the woods to a gate. Go through the gate, then turn left at the signpost and continue through the woods. Look out for the **River Chess**, down on your right as you walk. Go through a kissing gate to a signpost, then walk about 10m to a track. Turn right and walk along a surfaced track to a footbridge.

# THE CHILTERNS Year Round Walks

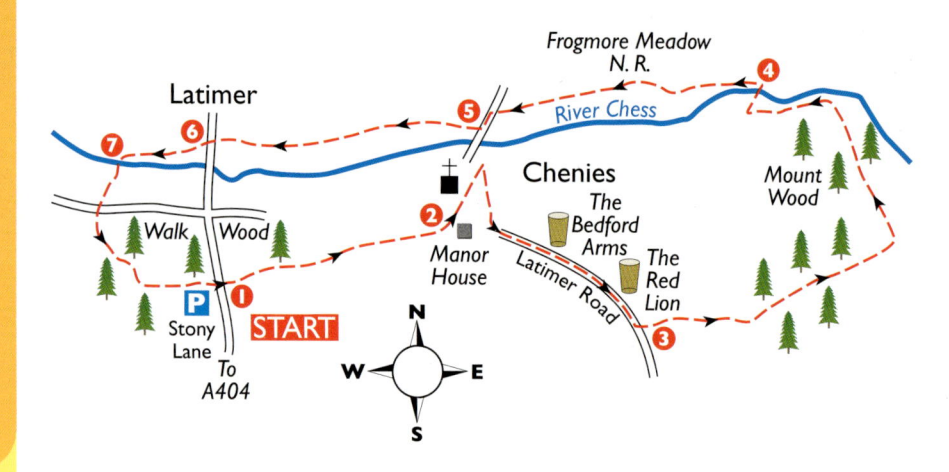

*summer*

**④** Cross the bridge, passing a barn on your right selling watercress and ice cream. Now take the left turn, signed **The Chess Valley Walk**, and follow the boardwalk. Pass a sign on your left about water voles, and a sign for **Frogmore Meadow Nature Reserve**. Walk through woods and a kissing gate, then cross a field and another kissing gate. The path leads you between fields with hills to your right, until eventually a metal gate leads you to **Chenies Hill**.

*Meeting some horses by the path in the Chess Valley.*

## Chenies and the Chess Valley

**5** Turn left and follow the narrow road past paddocks to **Mill Farm Barns**. Turn right here, through a metal gate, and follow the bridleway with watermeadows and the River Chess on your left. Stay on the bridleway, heading west and ignoring a path leading off on your right. At the end of the field, go through two metal gates to a lane.

**6** Turn right along the lane for about 10m, then go through a wooden kissing gate. You come to two paths across the field. Take the left option, walking by the banks of the river.

**7** Turn left over the bridge, then ahead through a kissing gate and across a field with a private drive on either side. Go through a kissing gate to a road. Cross the road, then through a metal gate to follow the path on your left by a fence towards the wood. Go through a kissing gate into the wood and follow the middle path, veering to the left and uphill. Ignore any cross paths. At the top of the path turn right to leave the wood. Then turn left and go through a metal kissing gate to follow a public footpath between fencing, until you come to a kissing gate and the parking area.

### What to look out for –

If you are very lucky, you might spot a water vole by the banks of the **River Chess**, as this is one of the last remaining strongholds in the Chilterns for this delightful mammal. The lush vegetation by the banks of the river provide water voles with both food and hiding places. Sadly, they are Britain's fastest declining mammal, threatened by both habitat loss and predation by the introduced American Mink. Water voles have chestnut-brown fur, a rounded nose, small rounded ears and, unlike a rat, a furry tail. Look out for their burrows in the riverbank, often with nibbled grass around the entrance. Kingfishers, brown trout and dragonflies also call this river home.

*The church and village of Hambleden.*

# 10 Hambleden Valley

**6.5 miles / 10.4km**

The Hambleden Valley is one of the most beautiful spots in the Chilterns, and sits just north of the River Thames. This walk includes a stretch along watermeadows by the Thames, before skirting the village of Medmenham and passing the earthworks of Medmenham Camp hillfort. This was part of a series of defended sites, established across the Chiltern Hills during the late Bronze Age and Iron Age. The return route enjoys far-reaching views across the fields, with the church and village of Hambleden on the horizon ahead of you, well worth exploring after the walk.

## The Walk

**1** From the car park, cross **Skirmett Road** and turn right towards **Mill End**. At the junction turn left, then walk for about 100m before crossing the road to walk up the track by the side of a cottage (number 23).

# Hambleden Valley

## The Facts

**Terrain** Some road walking on wide verges, but mainly fields, watermeadows and woodland. There are some steep sections, stiles and tree roots across the path so I would recommend decent walking shoes for this route.

**Map** OS Explorer 171 Chiltern Hills West and OS Explorer 172 Chiltern Hills East (although you could get away with just taking sheet 171).

**Starting point** The free car park on Skirmett Road. (GR SU 785855).

**How to get there & parking** Mill End is about three miles north-east of Henley. Follow the A4155, then turn onto Skirmett Road in the centre of Mill End. The free car park is on the left as you head north. **Sat nav:** RG9 6TL.

**Refreshments** You pass the Dog and Badger in Medmenham, which is a very old pub that has been refurbished into a luxury bar and restaurant. Walkers with muddy boots might prefer the seated area outside (thedogandbadger.com). In Hambleden, you'll find the Stag and Huntsman, which serves seasonal food and has a children's menu (thestagandhuntsman.co.uk).

*summer*

❷ The track veers left and turns into a grassy path, which leads you to **Ferry Lane**. Continue along the lane, with glimpses of the **Thames** across the field on your right. After a stretch, Ferry Lane turns right, but you stay ahead to follow the public footpath between hedges along a wide surfaced lane. Where the lane turns right, go through the kissing gate directly in front of you, then turn right to follow the path round the side of an arable field until you are walking with the Thames on your right.

❸ Go through a wooden gate and you come to some benches and a memorial. Cross the small footbridge just past the memorial, then walk up another **Ferry Lane**, with some very 'des res' properties on your right.

❹ Just before a small bridge with white railings, turn right to follow the public footpath with a small stream on your left. Go through a kissing gate to a narrow path with hedgerows on your right. Cross a footbridge then follow the footpath through a gate and diagonally across two fields, admiring the row of poplars on your right as you walk. Go through two gates to a drive, then turn left over a stone bridge to a road.

# THE CHILTERNS  Year Round Walks

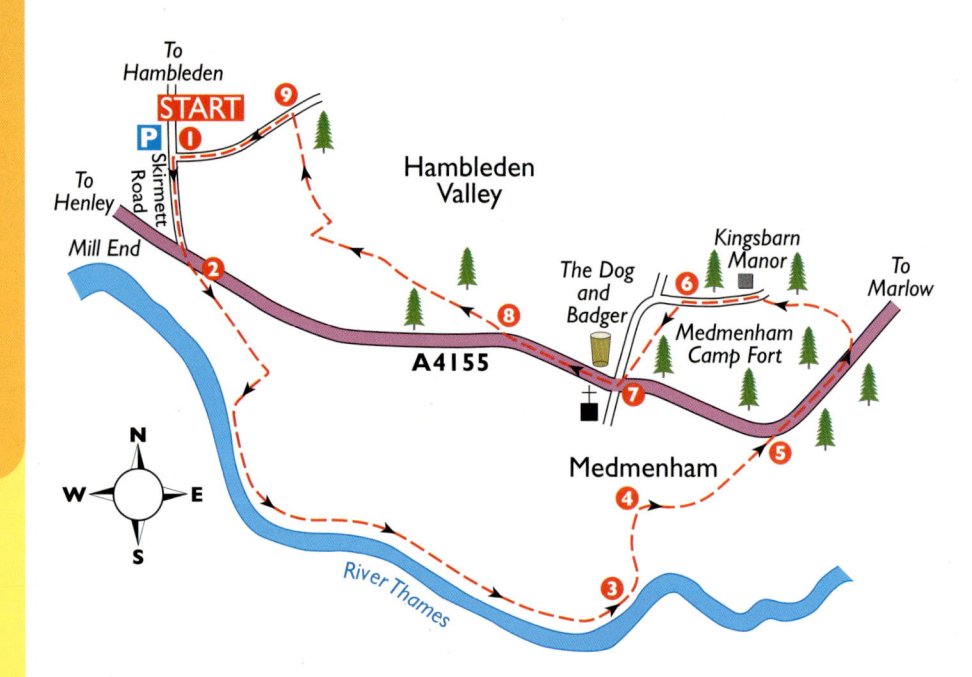

*summer*

⑤ Now turn right and walk with care along the verge by the side of the A4155. Cross just before **Danesfield House**, to follow the public bridleway down a surfaced track. Pass the drive to **Kingsbarn Manor** on your right and follow the footpath steeply uphill for a short stretch. Pass **The Pheasantry** on your right and walk straight on to follow the footpath. Stay on the path until you come to the drive in front of the gates to a house.

⑥ Turn right and follow the drive until you come to some cottages. Pass **The Old School House**, with the bell still proudly on display then, opposite its next door neighbour, turn left to follow the public footpath, passing a small orchard of ornamental cherry trees. Cross a drive, then almost immediately turn right into woods – don't go through the farm gate into the field. Pass an information board about **Medmenham Camp** Iron Age hillfort, and now follow the white arrows through the wood, staying on the main path heading roughly south. Look out for another information board about the camp, before the path leads steeply downhill to **Bockmer Lane**.

⑦ Cross the road to the church, then turn right, passing the **Dog and Badger** on your right, and walk along the pavement by the road. Just past the sign for **Medmenham**, cross the road to follow the public footpath through a metal kissing gate.

## Hambleden Valley

**8** The path winds uphill with woods on your left and a stunning view on your right across the fields. The path turns left into the woods and very shortly look out for a gap in the fence on your left. Now leave this main path and follow the narrower path with a steep slope down to your left. Cross a stile into a field then walk ahead along the bottom of the field. The path heads to the right, with the church at **Hambleden** soon visible on the horizon. When you come to a gravel track, cross it and follow the footpath across the next field. Cross two stiles, then walk straight on to the far corner of the field, where there is a metal kissing gate and a footpath sign.

**9** Go through the gate then turn left and follow the lane down to the main road and turn right for the car park (or go through the metal swing gate to walk to Hambleden).

### What to look out for –

**Hambleden** village is a delightful spot, and can be reached on foot at the end of the walk by following the footpath for about ¾ mile, or by car. There's a small car park in the village (follow the parking sign opposite the church). There are brick and flint cottages to admire, as well as the 12th-century St Mary the Virgin Church, an Elizabethan manor house, the Stag and Huntsman pub and a village shop. This idyllic village has been used as a filming location for *Midsomer Murders*, *Chitty Chitty Bang Bang* and *101 Dalmatians*. Hambleden manor house was the birthplace of the 7th Earl of Cardigan, who so disastrously led the Charge of the Light Brigade during the Crimean War, which left 247 men dead or wounded in the 'Valley of Death', as the riders hopelessly charged against Russian guns. Cardigan was also responsible for woollen, button-up jumpers that he introduced to keep his soldiers warm.

*autumn*

*Impressive views across the valley as you head up Pitstone Common.*

# 11 Ashridge Estate
### 6.8 miles / 10.9km

A stunning walk following the edge of the Ashridge Estate's beechwoods, with far-reaching views across the rolling Chiltern landscape, including Incombe Hole and the Ivinghoe Hills. You could also extend the walk by a mile for a 'there and back' trip to the top of Ivinghoe Beacon. The Ashridge Estate is managed by the National Trust and this walk starts by the towering granite Bridgewater Monument, where there is ample parking, a gift shop, café and toilets, making it a very useful starting point. If you have some energy left at the end of the walk, on weekends from April to October you can climb the Monument's 172 steps, to be rewarded with a view stretching as far as Waddesdon Manor and Wendover Woods. The area is very popular with local dog walkers, so if you have your four-legged friend with you they will have plenty of company. The Icknield Way leads you back towards fields grazed by sheep, so around point 6 they'll need to be on a lead. This landscape has been farmed for centuries, with grazing animals creating the perfect conditions for wild flowers and butterflies. Look out for the black wooden Pitstone Windmill, balanced on its white base as you walk. It is a very rare early form of a post mill, dating back to the early 17th century. The leaves in Ashridge blaze with colour in autumn, although it would be worth paying a visit in spring too, to see the woodland floor carpeted with bluebells.

## Ashridge Estate 11

*The Facts*

**Terrain**  You don't need to climb to admire the views on this walk as, other than a series of wooden steps at point 5, it is mainly level ground. The first section through the Ashridge Estate follows very well maintained gravel tracks that make walking easy at any time of the year. The return route through the woods is along a footpath that is also a bridleway, so can be muddy. There are no stiles or road walking.

**Map**  OS Explorer 181 Chiltern Hills North.

**Starting point**  Bridgewater Monument, Ashridge Estate. (GR SP 970131).

**How to get there & parking**  The National Trust Visitor Centre, and its free car park, is off the B4506 between Berkamsted and Dagnall. **Sat nav:** HP4 1LT.

**Refreshments**  Brownlow Café, next to the Visitor Centre, has a large outside seating area with some cover from the elements. They serve breakfast and lunch, delicious cakes and hot drinks, and dogs are allowed in this area (brownlowcafe.co.uk). There is often an ice cream and coffee van in the car park as well.

*autumn*

## The Walk

❶ Standing in front of the monument, turn right and follow the wide path signed '**Duncombe Terrace**'. Follow this main path straight on through **Pitstone Common**, crossing a wooden footbridge. The path starts to go uphill for a stretch, passing a sign on the right marking the end of the mobility route. Go through a gate next to **Clipperdown Cottage**.

❷ Turn left and follow the track, admiring the view on the left towards **Pitstone Hill**. Stay on this main path and soon you will spot Pitstone Windmill across the fields. Cross a cattle grid with a gate next to it, then almost immediately after this, take the left turn down a path, marked with a National Trust horseshoe.

❸ The path ends with a spectacular view ahead of you over **Incombe Hole**. Go through the gate on your left then turn immediately right to follow the **Ridgeway**, with the ground sloping away to your left. This narrow path leads you through an area of scrub from which you emerge to see the chalk path snaking up to **Ivinghoe Beacon** ahead of you. Look out for kestrels here, hanging in the air as they hunt for insects and small mammals in the chalk grasslands. Walk down to the road and cross with care as you are on a bend.

53

# THE CHILTERNS Year Round Walks

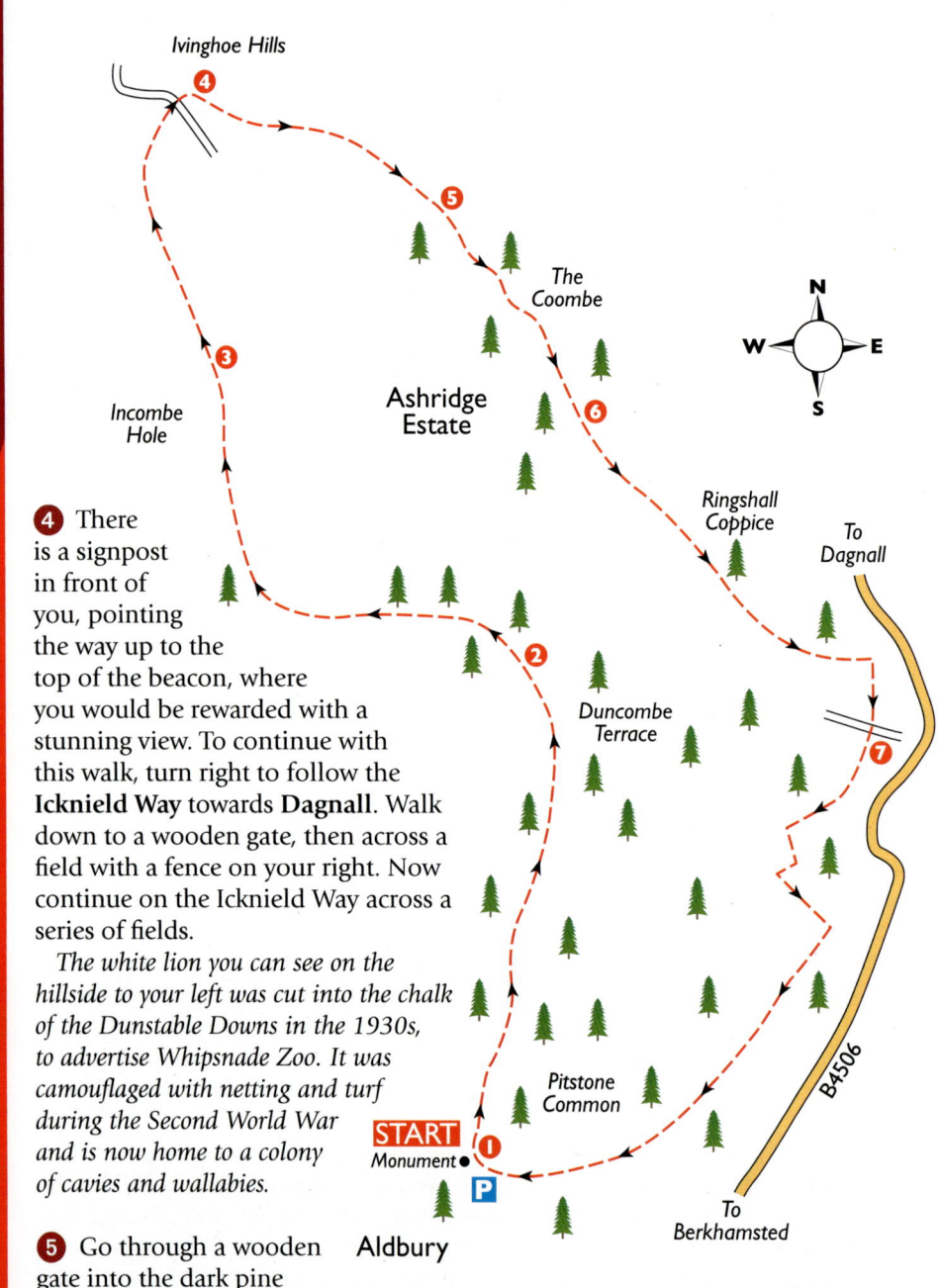

*autumn*

**4** There is a signpost in front of you, pointing the way up to the top of the beacon, where you would be rewarded with a stunning view. To continue with this walk, turn right to follow the **Icknield Way** towards **Dagnall**. Walk down to a wooden gate, then across a field with a fence on your right. Now continue on the Icknield Way across a series of fields.

*The white lion you can see on the hillside to your left was cut into the chalk of the Dunstable Downs in the 1930s, to advertise Whipsnade Zoo. It was camouflaged with netting and turf during the Second World War and is now home to a colony of cavies and wallabies.*

**5** Go through a wooden gate into the dark pine trees of **The Coombs**, then come to a short series of wooden steps that take you up to higher ground. Go through a swing gate, then cross the field to

## Ashridge Estate 11

another gate, with **Wards Hurst Farm** on your right.

**6** Now you leave the Icknield Way behind, and head straight on, following a public footpath to the left of a large shed. Walk across a series of fields, following the footpath signs. There are often sheep in these fields. Go through a wooden swing gate signed '**Ashridge Estate Boundary Trail**', then walk along a fenced path with **Ringshall Coppice** on your left. Go through another gate then walk by the side of a large field towards a house. Go through the gate and follow a wire fence round an underground reservoir, then down the concrete drive to the road.

**7** Cross the road to follow the public footpath through the woods, passing a car park on your right. Continue ahead as the path veers to the left. When you come to a cross track, turn right for about 100m, then at a junction of paths with a post on your left, turn left to follow the public footpath along a wide glade. When you can see a road ahead, turn right at the post and follow the public footpath, now heading south-west. When you come to another crosstrack, turn right and follow the purple sign for a short distance to arrive back at the monument.

*autumn*

### What to look out for –

The warmth of summer followed by autumn damp creates an explosion of mushrooms on the woodland floor and fallen logs. They are the fruiting part of fungi and appear throughout autumn to spread their spores. Some mushrooms are fatally poisonous, so better to admire them and leave them where they are rather than picking them. Fungi are nature's recycler, helping to decompose wood and return its nutrients back to the soil.

55

*Aldbury village and duck pond.*

# 12 Aldbury and the Grand Union Canal

### 9 miles / 14.4km

This is the ideal walk for an autumnal day in the countryside, starting from the picture-perfect village of Aldbury, complete with a duck pond, two characterful pubs and well-preserved stocks and whipping post. Aldbury is a lovely village to spend some time in and both of its pubs are highly recommended. It is easy to see why it is a popular location for film and television, and the village has appeared in many productions including *Inspector Morse*, *Midsomer Murders* and *The Dirty Dozen*. This route leads you along a rolling Chiltern escarpment to the Grand Union Canal. Then follows the towpath with the autumn colours reflected in the water, before passing two farms and heading up Pitstone Hill to the Ridgeway, leading you across Aldbury Nowers Nature Reserve. In autumn, the changing colour of the leaves fills the woods with seasonal colour, while squirrels and jays bury acorns for food through the cold winter. This is also a good option for dog walkers, as woodland and towpaths will keep you well away from roads and livestock. It crosses some farmland where signs request that dogs are on a lead.

## Aldbury and the Grand Union Canal    12

### The Facts

**Terrain**  The towpath is very easy walking in all weathers as this level surface is well maintained. There are two uphill sections and some wooden steps on the downward slopes. No stiles and only a very short section by a road.

**Map**  OS Explorer 181 Chiltern Hills North.

**Starting point**  The stocks by the village pond, Aldbury. (GR SP 964125).

**How to get there & parking**  Aldbury is between Aylesbury and Hemel Hempstead. From the A41, take the A4251 exit into the village. There is a small car park in the centre of Aldbury in front of the Greyhound pub and some parking spots round the pond. **Sat nav:** HP23 5RT.

**Refreshments**  There are two equally excellent pubs in Aldbury that both serve food: the Greyhound Inn (greyhoundaldbury.co.uk) and the Valiant Trooper (valianttrooper.co.uk).

## The Walk

**1** Head down **Trooper Road**, passing the **Valiant Trooper**, then straight on along **Berryfields** cul de sac. Follow the signed public footpath at the bottom, then walk through a swing gate and along a grassy path by the side of a field. Go through another swing gate and turn left, to follow the **Hertfordshire Way**.

**2** Cross a road and walk straight ahead, along the drive of some very impressive houses, following the sign for **Tom's Hill**. The path follows a brick wall, then hedges, until you come to a signpost. Now turn right, still following the **Hertfordshire Way**, and through a wooden fence gate to walk under the beech trees up Tom's Hill.

**3** When you come to a surfaced track in front of a triangle of grass, turn right to follow the **Chiltern Way** past houses, then through two farm gates into woods. The path heads downhill to another farm gate with a signpost on the other side. Go through the gate, then turn immediately left and head up to the top of the field and through a swing gate. Follow the Chiltern Way across the field and down to a gate. Go through the gate then down a series of wooden steps. Turn left to walk by a large arable field, then through a gate and across the land of **Norcott Court Farm**, passing the farm buildings to a drive.

# THE CHILTERNS  Year Round Walks

*autumn*

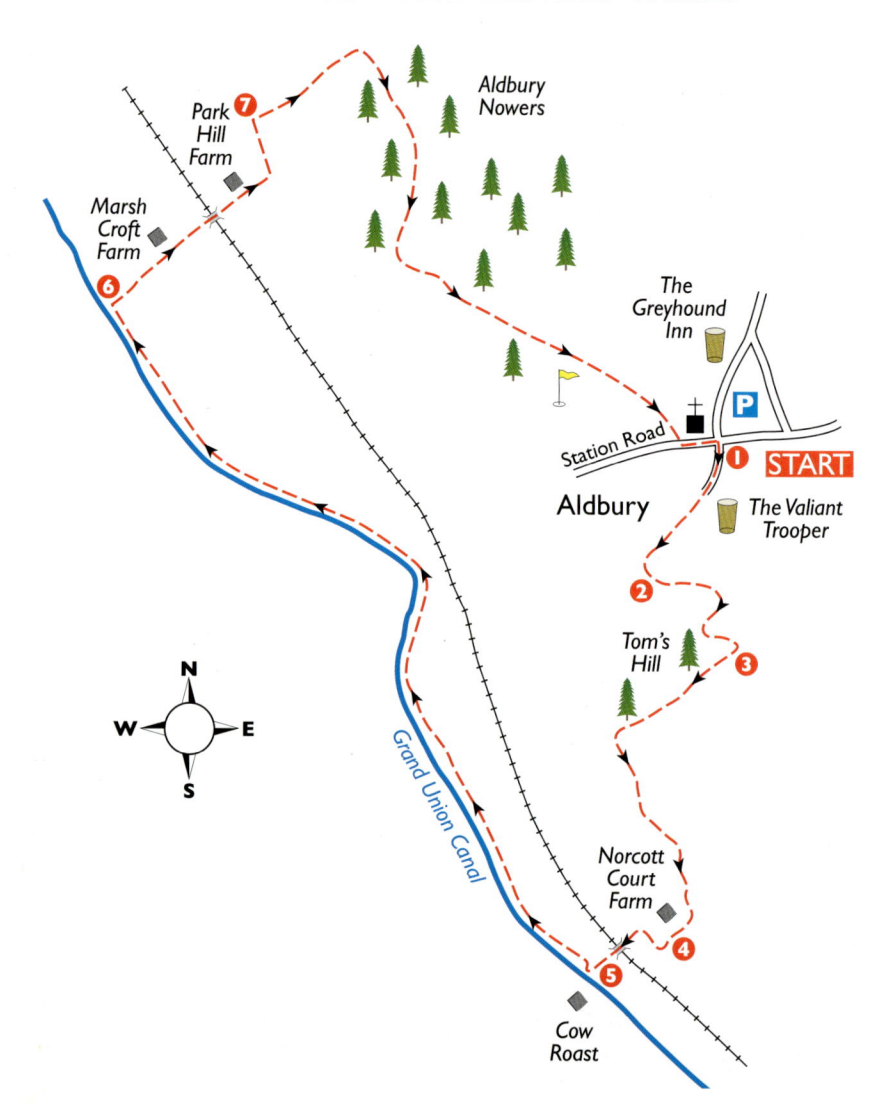

④ Cross the drive and, just to the right of the field in front of you (with a herd of very curious alpacas last time I passed), look out for the Chiltern Way sign, leading you by the side of the field and heading towards the canal. About three quarters of the way down the field, turn right at the Chiltern Way sign, then after about 100m, turn left to walk across a field and over a bridge to cross the railway line. Then walk down to a track, where you turn right.

⑤ Pass a sign for **Cowroast Marina**, then turn right onto the towpath by the

58

## *Aldbury and the Grand Union Canal*

**Grand Union Canal**. Now you have an easy stretch of walking for about three miles by the water, watching the occasional narrowboat chug past you.

**6** When the towpath leads up to a bridge and crosses to the other side of the canal, leave the water behind and turn right. Follow the drive of **Marsh Croft Farm**, with a view of **Pitstone Hill** ahead of you. The path takes you back over the train track and through a gate, to walk by **Park Hill Farm** to a road. Cross the road and turn left, there is a grass verge you can follow, then after the lay-by, a narrow path along the verge. The path up to Pitstone Hill is signed on the right.

**7** This is a steep section but well worth it, as it takes you up to **Aldbury Nowers Nature Reserve**, with some stunning views across the Chiltern valley. You meet the **Ridgeway**, then turn right to follow this ancient path through a swing gate into woods. Stay on the Ridgeway until you come to a path and another Ridgeway footpath sign. Now turn left, then about 50m further on, right, following the yellow arrow. You will soon see **Aldbury** ahead of you on the horizon. This path leads across a golf course, then through gates and past a large green shed. When you get to the village, turn left and walk down **Station Road**, past the 13th-century **St John the Baptist church** to the green.

*With less sunlight, the trees stop producing the chlorophyll needed for photosynthesis, and this creates the stunning autumn colours.*

# THE CHILTERNS Year Round Walks

## What to look out for –

*autumn*

The **Grand Union Canal** links London to Birmingham, passing the rolling Chilterns landscape, as well as peaceful villages and industrial towns. As its name suggests, it was formed from the amalgamation of several different canals. During the 19th century, the canals contributed to the industrial revolution by enabling heavy loads to be transported across the country. Narrowboats were originally wooden, and pulled by a horse walking along the towpath, led by a crew member, often a child. From the 1830s, as canals started to suffer competition from the new railways, the boatmen moved their families onboard. This saved them rent as well as providing extra hands to work the boats. This itinerant lifestyle meant that their children had no chance of receiving any education. By the end of the 19th century, the tradition of painting roses and castles on the boats was established and as you walk along the towpath, you can admire the narrowboats as they chug past you, for there is still plenty of life on the canal, with pleasure boats, walkers and cyclists all enjoying this tranquil spot.

*Beechwoods once provided the local furniture-making industry with wood.*

# 13 Nettlebed

**3 miles / 4.8km**

**T**he name 'Nettlebed' dates back to the 13th century, and simply means a place filled with nettles – but don't worry, this walk is instead filled with classic Chiltern beechwoods and magnificent tree tunnel paths. The statuesque beech thrive on the chalk soil of the Chilterns and Nettlebed is lucky enough to be surrounded by woods. This walk starts in the village, with its impressive Georgian houses, friendly pub and historic brick kiln, then heads off to explore the surrounding woodland. Look out for pits and hollows in the woods. These are the remains of sawpits, as it was more practical to saw large trunks into planks while still in the wood, before transporting them. Sawyers used a two-handled saw, with the 'under-dog' standing at the bottom of the pit, the sawdust falling into his eyes, and the 'top-dog' guiding the saw from above. There are also some quarry pits, which were dug to find clay and flint for house building. This woodland walk is an excellent choice for dog walkers, and the autumn colours are truly spectacular.

# THE CHILTERNS  Year Round Walks

**Terrain**  Mainly level walking along woodland paths, pavements in the village and a short section by the Watlington Road, which has no pavement, but you can easily walk along the verge. No stiles.

**Map**  OS Explorer 171 Chiltern Hills West.

**Starting point**  The White Hart pub. (GR SU 699867).

**How to get there & parking**  Nettlebed is 10 miles north of Reading, and on the A4130 as you head from Wallingford to Henley. The White Hart pub has a large car park behind it, which you could use if you are also visiting the pub but check with the landlord first. Otherwise, there is roadside parking round the village green. **Sat nav:** RG9 5DD.

**Refreshments**  The White Hart pub is a perfect spot for lunch and welcomes dogs and walkers inside, or in its pretty garden (tmdining.co.uk/the-white-hart.html).

## The Walk

**1** With your back to the pub, turn right and walk down **Nettlebed High Street** until you come to the church on your left. Just past the church, turn right and follow the footpath gently uphill, passing allotments.

*Autumn colours are at their best after hot, dry summers.*

# Nettlebed 13

*autumn*

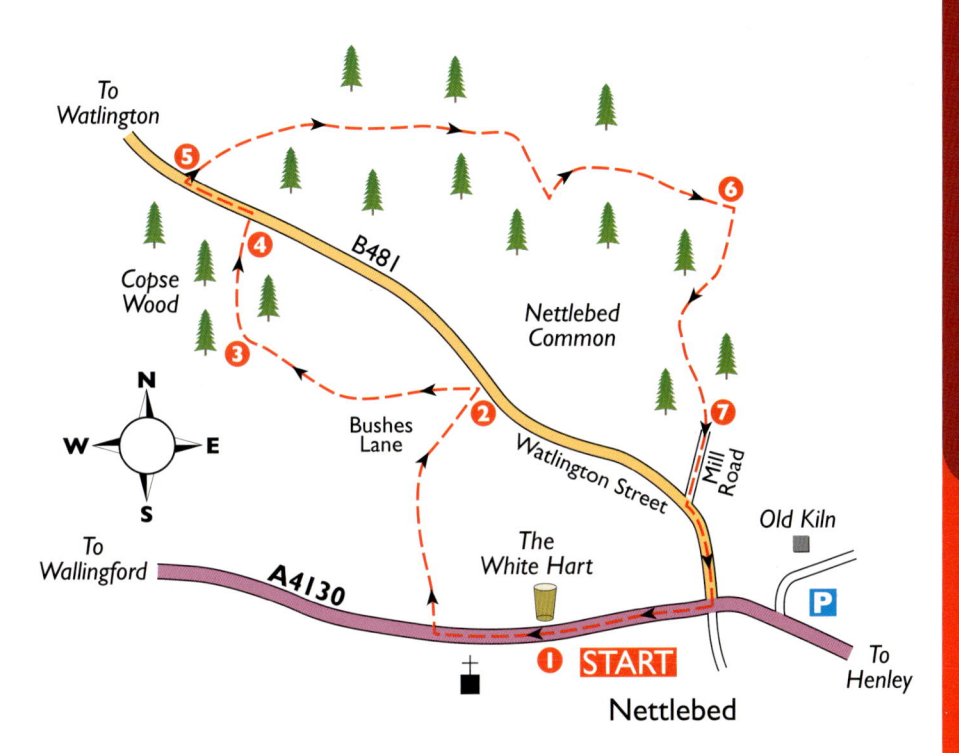

**2** The footpath comes out onto **Watlington Street**. Don't go up to the road, instead take the left turn to follow the restricted byway sign between hedgerows with the road on your right. This is **Bushes Lane** and it leads you out of Nettlebed to the woods. You shortly come to a 'V' junction, take the left turn and follow the narrow path with houses on your right at first, then a lovely view across the fields.

**3** Bushes Lane leads you to a surfaced lane with a field on your left. You need to go forward a few metres and turn right, following a footpath into **Copse Wood**. From this point onwards, look out for white arrows painted on the trees, as they will show you are on the right tracks.

**4** The trees end and there is a patch of scrub and blackberry bushes between you and the B481 (Watlington Road). You will be able to hear the road, but depending on the time of year, you can either follow a narrow path directly ahead through the bushes, or turn right until there is an easier way through the trees. But once on the road, take care as there are no pavements. Turn left and follow the road for about 200m until you see a 30mph sign at the edge of **Park Corner** village.

63

# THE CHILTERNS  Year Round Walks

**5** Now turn right and follow the footpath sign back into the woods, heading north-east. You will find yourself walking along a majestic avenue of ancient beech trees that arch over the path. At a path junction, take the route on the right and walk down to an unsurfaced lane. Turn left, then just before the cattle grid, turn right and follow the path with the fenceline on your left.

**6** You come to a very large house and an unsurfaced road. Walk straight on past this house, and its next-door neighbour, to walk back into woods. The footpath is on your left, signed by a white arrow on a tree. Follow the path until you come out of the woods to **Mill Road**.

**7** Turn right and walk downhill back towards **Nettlebed**. When you come to **Watlington Street**, turn left and walk down to the **High Street**, then right to return to the pub (or left if you are parked by the green, or want to visit the **Old Kiln**).

## What to look out for –

Nettlebed's economy was based around brickmaking from the 14th century until the 1930s. One remaining pottery kiln has been preserved in the village and is worth having a look at. The 17th-century bottle-shaped kiln once fired 18,000 bricks at a time, and is now the only bottle kiln, of this period and design, left in the country. Clay for the bricks came from Nettlebed Common, and a stroll down Nettlebed High Street will show you what the finished bricks looked like. There is an information board by the kiln with more information on its history.

*autumn*

*These famous woods have had a starring role in* **Robin Hood Prince of Thieves, The Crying Game, First Knight** *and* **Ivanhoe.**

# 14 Burnham Beeches

### 3 miles / 4.8km

This well-managed National Nature Reserve is home to 220 hectares of ancient beech and oak pollards, with the resulting range of flora and fauna that such a landscape supports. It's an important conservation area, with the reserve taking care to look after its dead as well as living wood. Deadwood is an important natural habitat, providing food and shelter for rare wildlife. Burnham Beeches is also a popular spot with dog walkers, although be aware of the restrictions where your hound can be on or off lead (maps by the car park show this information). Lots of information boards make this walk easy to navigate, and there is no shortage of friendly dog walkers who are keen to point you in the right direction. Look out for the gnarled, 800-year-old Druid's Oak near the start of the route, as well as an Iron Age hillfort and medieval moated farmstead, which are all passed on this perfect autumnal stroll.

# THE CHILTERNS  Year Round Walks

**Terrain**  Mainly level, with a small gradient towards the end. This route follows tarmac tracks through the woods, with a few stretches under the trees along woodland paths. Horses and cyclists aren't allowed off the tarmac roads, therefore the paths are always in a good condition, even after wet weather. No stiles.

**Map**  OS Explorer 172 Chiltern Hills East.

**Starting point**  The Beeches Café on Lord Mayor's Drive. (GR SU 954850).

**How to get there & parking**  Burnham Beeches lies between Slough and Beaconsfield. From the A355, turn down Lord Mayor's Drive and follow the road a short distance to the main car park. There is a £3 charge on Saturdays and Sundays for all-day parking. **Sat nav:** SL2 3LB.

**Refreshments**  The Beeches Café serves hot drinks and refreshments. There are various outside seating options and an area for dog owners.

## The Walk

**1** With your back to the café, turn left and follow the tarmac track of **Lord Mayor's Drive**. An alternative path runs parallel to the drive on your left, passing Upper and Middle Pond. Both paths pass the 800-year-old Druid's Oak before arriving at a gate and small cattle grid at Seven Ways Crossing, and the site of an Iron Age hillfort.

*Burnham Beeches was bought by the Corporation of London in 1880, saving it from developers, with Victoria Drive named after the Queen.*

# *Burnham Beeches* 14

*autumn*

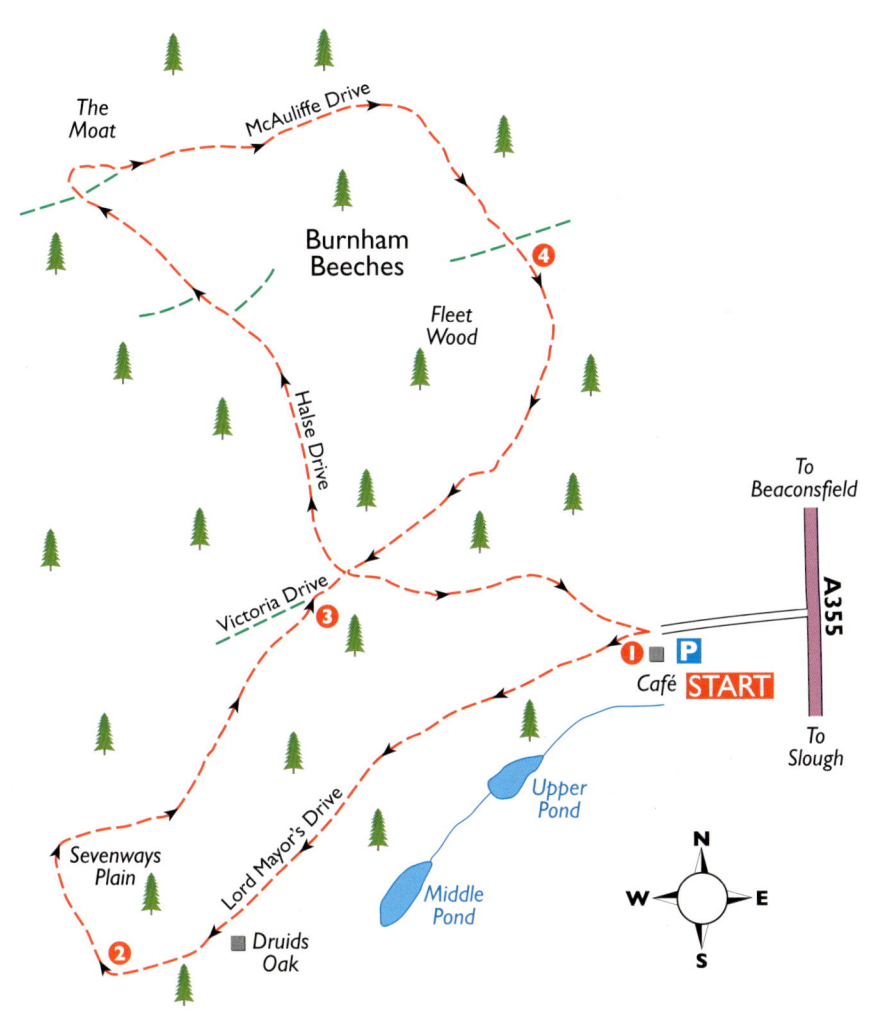

**2** Go through the gate and turn directly right, following the path between the hut and the fence. Now follow the path through the woods, keeping the fence on your right, until you come to a path leading off in each direction. There's a gate at the end of a short path to your right, but you need to turn left here, and head downhill for a short distance to join a wide, flat path.

**3** This is **Victoria Drive**. Turn right and walk about 20m to **Halse Drive**. Turn left and follow the tarmac route uphill. This path ends by the northern edge of Burnham Beeches, by **The Moat**. Turn right and follow **McAuliffe Drive**, taking time to look at the information board which explains the background to the medieval moated farmstead that you are walking beside.

# THE CHILTERNS  Year Round Walks

**④** When you come to a cross track, with a large Burnham Beeches sign on your right, go straight ahead, leaving the tarmac track to follow the woodland path. Pass a cross track and continue ahead until you arrive back on **Halse Drive**. Now turn left and walk a short and slightly uphill stretch back to the café and car park.

## What to look out for –

There has been woodland here since the last Ice Age, with the landscape managed through the centuries by grazing lifestock beneath the pollarded trees. Pollarding is when the branches are regularly cut above head height in order to produce more wood and increase the lifespan of the tree. The most magnificent example of an ancient pollarded tree is the Druid's Oak. With a girth of around 9m, this pedunculate oak is the oldest tree in Burnham Beeches, estimated at around 800 years old. According to legend, Mendelssohn wrote some of the music for *A Midsummer Night's Dream* while visiting these woods.

*Temple Island and autumn leaves reflected in the still waters of the Thames.*

# 15 Henley-on-Thames
## 8 miles / 12.8km

This walk starts in historic Henley-on-Thames, with its Georgian town houses and 18th-century stone bridge. It then follows a section of the Oxfordshire Way, offering glorious views almost from the start. A quiet country lane takes you into the hamlet of Fawley, before you head off through impressive beechwoods, ablaze with colour in autumn. The final stretch follows the banks of the Thames as you return to Henley. The whole route is very easy to navigate, and there are plenty of tempting pubs and cafés for a well-earned treat at the end.

# THE CHILTERNS  Year Round Walks

*autumn*

*The Facts*

**Terrain**  There are only a few muddy sections on this walk and it is mainly easy walking along surfaced tracks and woodland paths. There are some up and downhill sections but no stiles. The footbridges that lead you to the Thames have handrails but are single-plank width, so I would not recommend doing this walk with a pushchair. Dobson's Lane does have the occasional car, but this is a popular walking area so they travel slowly.

**Map**  OS Explorer 171 Chiltern Hills West.

**Starting point**  The Dry Leas pay and display car park by the rugby club. (GR SU 760832).

**How to get there & parking**  Henley-on-Thames is nine miles north-east of Reading. Head for the northern edge of town, on the A4155 Marlow Road. The Dry Leas car park is right next to the rugby club. All the main car parks are clearly signed, in case there are no spaces left here on a match day. **Sat nav:** RG9 2JA.

**Refreshments**  There are plenty of options in Henley-on-Thames and it is a lovely town to explore. The Angel on the Bridge is a very welcoming pub with a terrace and river view (theangelhenley.com).

## The Walk

**1** From the car park, turn right and walk down to the roundabout. Then turn right to walk along the A4130 for about 400m. The footpath sign is immediately after the **Rupert House Playing Fields** on your right. Follow the **Oxfordshire Way** public footpath, looking out for the odd yellow arrow to keep you in the right direction. The path leads uphill, and when the fence ends on your right, continue uphill through **Little Wood** to a kissing gate. Go through the gate and keep going in the same direction until you come to a drive. This leads you past some houses before turning into a track. Stay on the Oxfordshire Way until you come to a country road with **Pond Cottage** on your right.

**2** Now turn right and follow **Dobson's Lane** to **Fawley**. Walk through the village, passing **St Mary the Virgin church** and the village green. Just past the green is a sign, where you go straight on in the same direction.

**3** When the road curves to the left by **Round House**, take the public footpath ahead, passing a house on your left. This path leads you into the magnificent

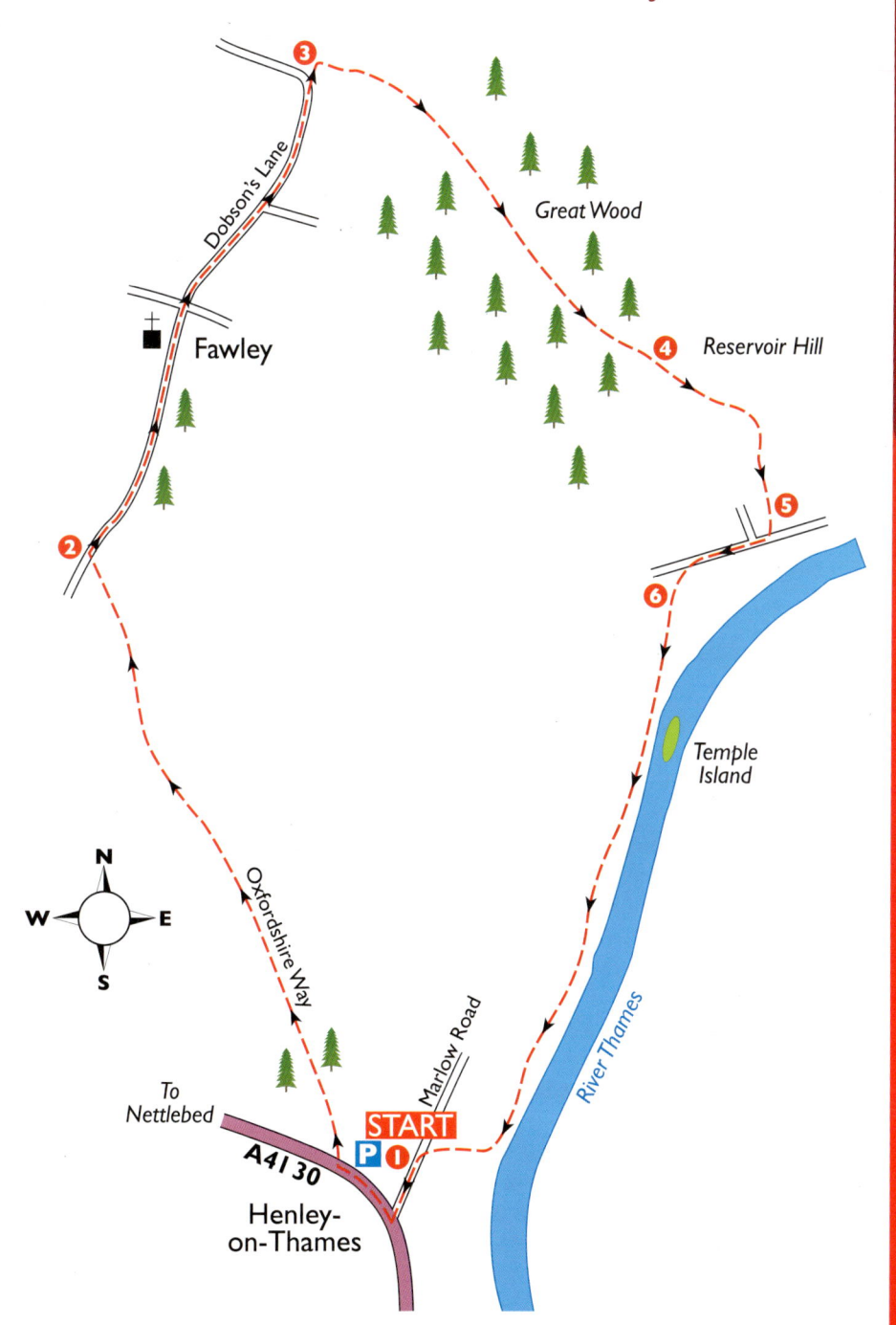

# Henley-on-Thames

**15**

*autumn*

Great Wood

Dobson's Lane

Fawley

❶ ❷ ❸ ❹ Reservoir Hill ❺ ❻

Temple Island

River Thames

Oxfordshire Way

Marlow Road

START
P ❶

To Nettlebed

A4130

Henley-on-Thames

N W E S

71

# THE CHILTERNS  Year Round Walks

*autumn*

*Standing at the top of Reservoir Hill, at point 4.*

**Great Wood**. The beech trees are widely spaced out so sometimes the actual footpath isn't clear. But keep walking in the same direction, heading south-east and looking out for the odd footpath sign or white arrow on a tree.

**4** You emerge from the woods at the top of **Reservoir Hill**, with silvery glimpses of the **Thames** in the valley below you. Follow the path down and at a cross track and public bridleway sign, turn right and walk through a gate and straight on. Follow this path through another gate and walk down to the main road.

**5** Turn right and walk about 10m along the verge, then cross with care to follow the footpath on the other side of the road. You will soon come to a kissing gate and footpath sign.

**6** Go through the gate. If you have a dog with you, watch out for sheep in these fields. Head half right, crossing a drive, then follow a series of narrow footbridges across the fields. You will then find yourself by **Temple Island** and the River Thames. Turn right and follow the river back towards **Henley**. As you reach the edge of town, turn left and follow the path to **Marlow Road**. Then turn left and cross the road back to the car park.

# Henley-on-Thames

## What to look out for –

You can't walk in the Chilterns without spotting the **red kites** as they effortlessly glide through the skies around you. In fact, it is hard to imagine the Chilterns without them, but they were only reintroduced to this country between 1989 and 1994. By the end of the 19th century, these magnificent birds of prey had been driven to extinction in England due to human persecution, with only a small population surviving in Wales. They were killed due to a mistaken belief that they took lambs and game birds, while in fact the kites scavenge on dead animals, and hunt small mammals, beetles and worms. Due to the hard work of the RSPB and English Nature, breeding pairs of kites were brought over from Spain and released into the Chilterns where they are now thriving. They are easy to identify, with a reddish-brown body, angled wings and a forked tail.

*autumn*

*winter*

*Brunel's arched Gatehampton Railway Bridge, built in 1838, carries the Great Western main line over the Goring Gap.*

# 16 Goring and the Thames Path

**4 miles / 6.4km**

The best views of the river are halfway round the walk, from a wooden bench at the top of Hartslock Nature Reserve. This is one of the finest picnic spots you can hope for. In June, the sloping grassland provides the perfect habitat for monkey orchids, and as the summer continues, the whole hillside becomes carpeted with wild marjoram. In winter, you can watch the kites soaring over the hill. The return stretch takes you along watermeadows by the bank of the winding Thames, then back to bustling Goring, with its excellent choice of charming pubs and cafés.

## *Goring and the Thames Path*   16

### The Facts

**Terrain** The first half of the walk is along surfaced paths, so perfect for a winter's day. The whole walk is level, except for a short climb. If there has been very heavy rain, then the meadows by the Thames on the second half of the walk might be flooded. There are no stiles on this walk.

**Map** OS Explorer 171 Chiltern Hills West.

**Starting point** Wheel Orchard pay and display car park in Goring. (GR SU 599806).

**How to get there & parking** Goring is 10 miles north-west of Reading. The B4009 and B4526 take you through Goring and the pay and display car park is clearly signed on Station Road. **Sat nav:** RG8 9HB.

**Refreshments** There is nothing en route, but there are plenty of options in Goring. You can get excellent picnic food at the Goring Grocer (goringgrocer.co.uk) at the start of the walk, you also pass Pierreponts (pierreponts.co.uk) at the end of the walk, that has tables outside. If you are looking for a pub, the Catherine Wheel (tcwgoring.co.uk) near the car park is Goring's oldest pub and has a charming beer garden, or across the bridge in Streatley is the Swan (theswanatstreatley.com).

*winter*

## The Walk

**❶** From the pay and display sign, turn left and walk down the narrow lane. This takes you to the **High Street**, opposite the **Goring Grocer** – so perfect for above-average picnic food! Cross the road and turn right, then keep going following the pavement and crossing the railway bridge.

*Wrapped up well for a winter's day.*

# THE CHILTERNS *Year Round Walks*

*winter*

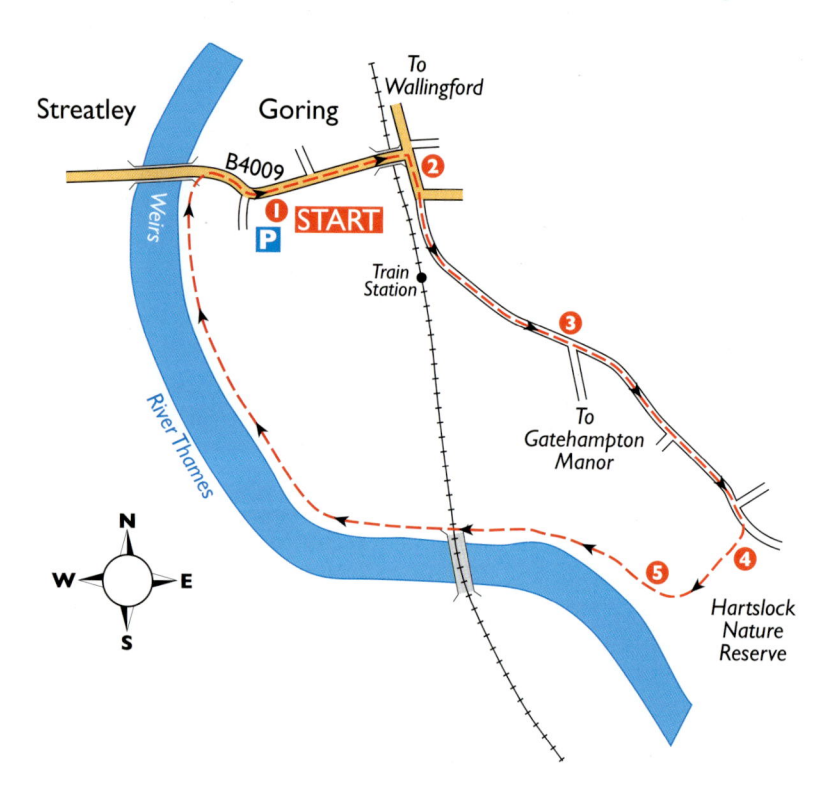

**②** At the junction, cross the road and head right along **Wallingford Road**, passing the train station and its car park on your right. Walk past the recreation ground on your left, then past houses until the pavement ends and you have fields on either side. If you have a dog with you, it is safe to be off lead, but watch out for the odd horse rider.

**③** Pass a '**Private Drive**' and sign to **Gatehampton Manor** on your right, and keep ahead, following the sign to Gatehampton House on the lane signed 'Unsuitable for motor vehicles'. Pass **Gatehampton Cottages** on your right and keep walking with hills to your left and the **Thames** down on your right. You eventually come to a junction with a farm gate on your right. Leave the lane now and take the bridleway on your right, walking with hedgerows either side. This pretty path leads you to the entrance to **Hartslock Nature Reserve** on your right.

**④** Go through the wooden gate, where there is a map of the nature reserve on an information board. Where you are heading to is a gate and another information board on the opposite side of the small hill in front of you. There

## Goring and the Thames Path 16

is a bench on top of the hill with a wonderful view of **Goring Gap**, there's also a gate at the top leading into the rest of the nature reserve if you want to stop awhile and explore. If you don't have the energy, or the ground is muddy after rain, turn right and follow the fence around the hill to the gate. I like to walk up the hill, stop at the top for a picnic, watch the kites swooping below me and the trains crossing Brunel's railway bridge, then back down the other side to the gate.

**5** Go through the gate and follow the **Thames Path**, passing horse paddocks, to the river. Now turn right and walk riverside for 1.5 miles back to **Goring**. Pass **Goring Lock** moorings, and when you get to the bridge, turn right and follow the Thames Path sign, passing **Goring Mill** on your left. Then walk back along the **High Street** to the lane on your right, leading back to the car park.

*winter*

## What to look out for –

The **Goring Gap** is the dramatic point where the Thames cut through the chalk of the Chiltern Hills during the last Ice Age, half a million years ago. Up to that moment, the Thames hadn't passed through Goring, Oxford or even London. Instead, it had turned north-east and reached the sea via East Anglia. But at some point during the Ice Age, the flow of the water was blocked by massive ice sheets, which forced a new route through the soft chalk of the hills, forming the Goring Gap. The river is narrower at this point, with the hills sweeping up on either side and it has always been an important crossing point, while archaeological finds such as flint blades and reindeer bones prove that Goring has been inhabited for at least 10,000 years. From the top of Hartslock Nature Reserve there are magnificent views of the Thames. The sloping grassland is also a good spot for wild flowers.

77

*winter*

*Cottages in The Lee.*

# 17 The Lee and Lee Common

### 3 miles /4.8km

An easy stroll along lanes and fields between the idyllic Chiltern villages of The Lee, Lee Clump and Lee Common. This walk is a good distance for families, and there's an excellent adventure playground in Lee Common which will be a highlight for younger walkers. Arable fields and quiet lanes will appeal to dog walkers, while the Cock and Rabbit overlooking the village green in The Lee is the quintessential English pub – with regular appearances in television's *Midsomer Murders*. The green itself is surrounded by brick and flint cottages, making this special part of the Chilterns a spot you'll be sure to return to in all seasons.

## The Lee and Lee Common

*The Facts*

**Terrain** The start of the walk follows pavements, then field paths for the second half. All level walking with a few stiles.

**Map** OS Explorer 181 Chiltern Hills North.

**Starting point** Roadside parking on Lee Clump Road. (GR SP 905043).

**How to get there & parking** The Lees are halfway between Wendover and Great Missenden, and can be reached via the A413, turning off to follow Leather Lane, then King's Lane, before heading west through The Lee along Lee Clump Road. Park roadside on Lee Clump Road, there is space just by the parish hall and shop. **Sat nav:** HP16 9JH.

**Refreshments** The Cock and Rabbit in Lee has an idyllic village location and serves delicious food with an Italian influence (graziemille.co.uk).

*winter*

## The Walk

**1** From **Lee Clump Road** turn down quiet **Oxford Street**, heading south-east, passing pretty cottages, then **Lee Common Primary School**. Look out for a telephone box tucked into the hedgerow on your right, and about 50m further on, turn right through a gate to follow the footpath past allotments, passing a bench and the adventure playground.

**2** Go through a gate, cross a lane by **Garden Cottage**, and straight on through the kissing gate to walk by the side of a small field. Go through another kissing gate and across the next field. Look out for gates on either side at the bottom of this field, with woodland beyond. Head for the gate on the right. At the metal swing gates, ignore the footpath on your left (which follows the direction of the telegraph poles), instead take the footpath straight on through the trees, heading north-west. Follow the wide path through the woods.

**3** When you come to a surfaced lane and footpath sign, turn right, following the '**Chiltern Link**' with a field on your left and some very impressive houses on your right. Come to a crossroads in **The Lee**, with the **Cock and Rabbit** on the corner in front of you.

**4** Turn right, then left in front of the pub, and walk by the edge of the village green. At the corner of the green, turn left by **Daffodil Cottage** and pass **St John the Baptist Church** on your left.

# THE CHILTERNS Year Round Walks

*winter*

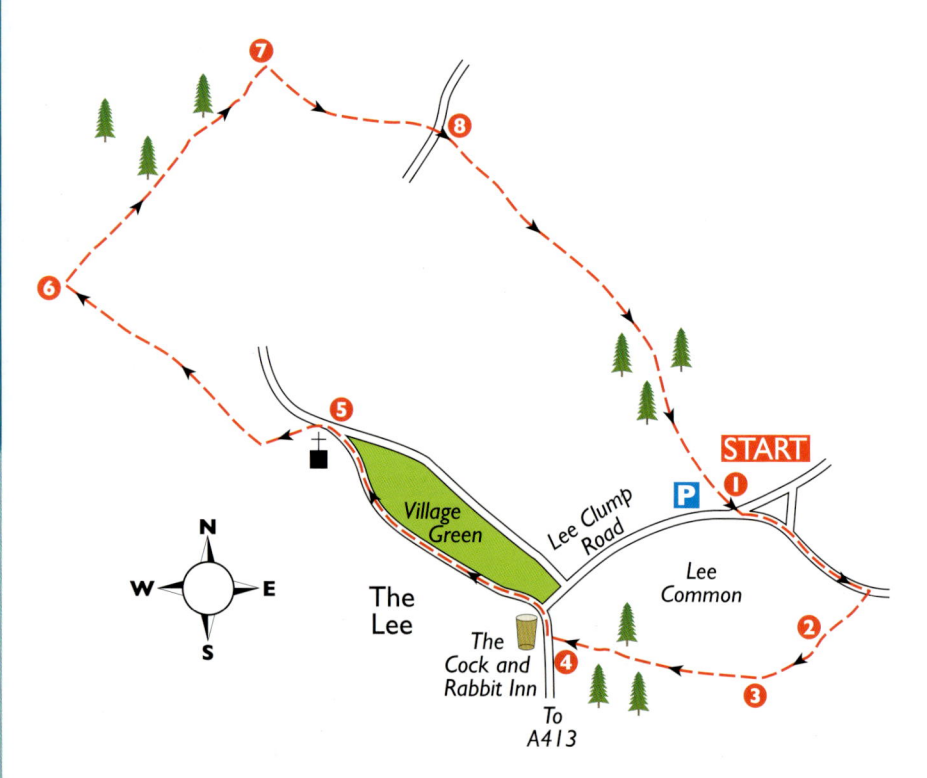

**⑤** Look out for a **Chiltern Link footpath sign** on your left by a stile, (just past a metal farm gate on the other side of the road, if you come to 'Lee Croft' you've missed it). Cross the stile and walk across a small field, to another stile. Cross a gravel drive between two cottages, then cross the stile and veer right across a field. Cross the stile next to a metal farm gate and at a junction of paths, follow the Chiltern Link arrow ahead, by the side of a large arable field with a hedge on your left. Keep on into the next field, with the hedge now on your right. Halfway along this field, look out for a public footpath sign on your right.

**⑥** Turn right here through a wide gap in the hedgerow and walk with an arable field on your left and hedgerow on your right. Continue into the next field, then the path veers left through trees, before leading you back to the side of another field.

**⑦** You come to another stile with a wide gap next to it and the house '**Rabbs Corner**' on your right. Turn right here and follow the gravel drive, which becomes paved for a stretch. You will see a large white house ahead of you, then come to a road.

## The Lee and Lee Common  17

*winter*

*Bare winter trees make excellent climbing frames to keep younger walkers entertained.*

81

# THE CHILTERNS  Year Round Walks

**8** Cross the road and follow the footpath ahead, through blackberry bushes. Pass a footpath post and keep going in the same direction. At a fork in the path, take the option on your left and continue through the woods, ignoring any side paths. You come out of the woods and into a large field. Follow the footpath diagonally across the field, heading under the telegraph wires. Go through the metal gate then head down to the road and your car.

## What to look out for –

Its picturesque villages, dotted with flint and brick cottages, just as much as its beech-topped hills and valleys, add to the mix of ingredients that make the Chilterns such a special place to be. The Lee is an idyllic spot at any time of year, with houses dating back to the 16th and 17th centuries. The Lees are at the heart of the Chilterns and well worth spending some time exploring.

*Ferry Lane leads you directly to the banks of the Thames.*

# 18 Medmenham and the River Thames

### 3 miles / 4.8km

**M**edmenham is a tiny village in a wonderful location, with Ferry Lane where this walk starts, leading straight down to the banks of the Thames. Until the Second World War, you could catch a ferry at this spot, where the Thames towpath crossed from the Buckinghamshire to the Berkshire side of the river. There follows a peaceful stretch by sheep-grazed meadows by the banks of the Thames. In spring, children will love watching the lambs and listening to their high-pitched bleats. The return journey is across fields with good views of the Chiltern Hills and plenty of chalk visible in the ploughed fields, evidence of how this landscape has been formed. In Medmenham, the charming 12th-century church of St Peter and St Paul is built with Chiltern chalk blocks and flint rubble and is worth a visit, while across the road the Dog and Badger serves hungry walkers with breakfast, lunch and dinner.

# THE CHILTERNS Year Round Walks

**Terrain** This walk is all level with no stiles. Ferry Lane is surfaced while the middle section of the walk by the Thames is on short grass. The return journey crosses some fields so could be muddy after rain.

**Map** OS Explorer 171 Chiltern Hills West.

**Starting point** St Peter and St Paul Church, Medmenham. (GR SU 804844).

**How to get there & parking** Medmenham is on the A4155, halfway between Marlow and Henley-on-Thames. Park roadside on Ferry Lane, there's normally a spot near the church. The pub also has a large car park, but check with the landlord before leaving your car. **Sat nav:** SL7 2HF.

**Refreshments** The Dog and Badger is more of a restaurant than a pub now, but you can still buy a pint and sit outside with a dog and hopefully not too muddy boots, and there are patio heaters and fleece blankets for chillier days (thedogandbadger.com). Another option is one of the various benches you pass on the route, where you can picnic with a riverside view.

## The Walk

① With the church on your right, walk down **Ferry Lane** towards the river. You pass various picturesque cottages, as well as the former vicarage and village post

*The Medmenham Ferry Memorial, built in 1936, proudly stands by the banks of the river commemorating Lord Devonport's 1899 defence of the public right-of-way over the ferry.*

# Medmenham and the River Thames  18

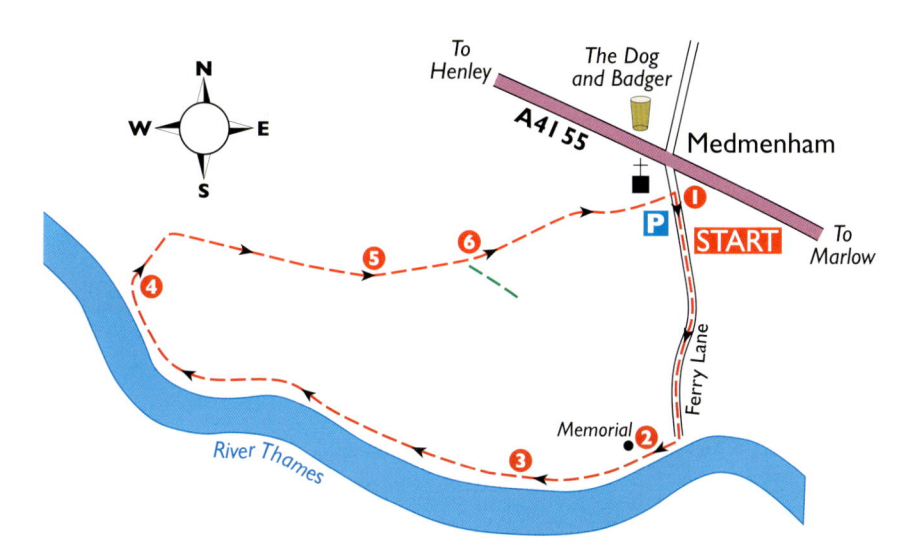

*winter*

office. The pavement very soon ends, but the only traffic along this lane is from the people lucky enough to live here.

**2** When you get to the end, with the river right in front of you, cross the short footbridge on your right, then turn right and follow the public footpath with the river directly on your left, passing **Medmenham Ferry Memorial**.

**3** Go through the gate (for the next stretch, if you have a dog with you it will probably need to be on a lead because there are often sheep here). Now just keep following the river bank as you cross the meadow, through another gate and across the next meadow to a gate right by the water's edge. This leads you to a field which you cross straight over to the other side and a wooden fence by a large thatched house.

**4** Now turn right and follow the public footpath for about 200m until you spot a metal kissing gate on your left that leads to a lane. There are two footpath arrows on a post by the gate, and the walk turns right to cross the field you are in, heading for the brick building you can see on the other side of the field, keeping the telegraph poles on your right.

**5** Cross the track and go straight across the next field, following the footpath and now walking under the telegraph wires, then across one more track and another field. You will now see a post in the field with two choices of path.

**6** Take the path heading left which will lead you across the field to a junction

85

# THE CHILTERNS  Year Round Walks

of paths. Go through the metal gate in front of you, then over the track and straight on, following a narrow footpath. Shortly, you'll see the 14th-century tower of **Medmenham's church** (the chancel and tower were built after the main building), before emerging back onto **Ferry Lane**.

## What to look out for –

Medmenham has some very pretty cottages and a stroll down Ferry Lane gives you a chance to admire them as you pass. The use of local materials has given the Chiltern villages a distinctive character. Flint is a traditional local building material, it is harder than chalk and was formed millions of years ago from silica in the remains of sponge-like creatures that lived in the sea that once covered this area.

Grazing sheep do an important job in the Chilterns, maintaining the chalk grassland ecosystem. By nibbling off the young shoots, they stop the saplings from growing into larger bushes and trees that would block the sunlight and take the limited water and nutrients from the soil. This give grasses, herbs and flowering plants the space to thrive on the open chalk grassland. These flowers in turn attract rare butterflies.

*Admiring the boats at Bourne End Marina.*

*winter*

# 19 Bourne End and Spade Oak Lake

### 3 miles / 4.8km

After admiring the boats in the marina, this walk takes you right by the banks of the Thames, with stunning views across the water to the Chiltern hills and chalk grasslands of Cock Marsh. This landscape was the inspiration for *The Wind in the Willows*, and the author, Kenneth Grahame, lived right across the water in Cookham.

You leave the river to explore the shady banks of Spade Oak Lake, where a short diversion takes you to the delightful village of Little Marlow. There are plenty of classic flint and brick cottages to admire, as well as the 16th-century Queens Head pub, with roses climbing round the porch, wooden beams and a welcoming fire making it well worth a visit.

# THE CHILTERNS Year Round Walks

*winter*

## The Facts

**Terrain** Level easy walking on grassy footpaths, starting and finishing in Bourne End.

**Map** OS Explorer 172 Chiltern Hills East.

**Starting point** The Parade, Bourne End. (GR SU 893873).

**How to get there & parking** Bourne End is six miles south of High Wycombe, off the A404. At the southern end of The Parade is Station Road and the train station. There is parking on the residential roads further down this road, or the station car park which charges £2.20 per day at the weekends. **Sat nav:** SL8 5QQ.

**Refreshments** In Little Marlow, the Queens Head is in an idyllic location and serves food every day (marlowslittlesecret.co.uk/#1).

## The Walk

**1** From **The Parade** in the centre of Bourne End, turn down **Wharf Lane**, which is almost opposite the filling station. This road leads down to the **Thames Path**.

**2** Turn right once you reach the river, passing the marina then the **Upper Thames Sailing Club** where there are picnic tables if you want to stop awhile and admire the view across the water. Walk across **Spade Oak Meadow**, then go through the metal kissing gate.

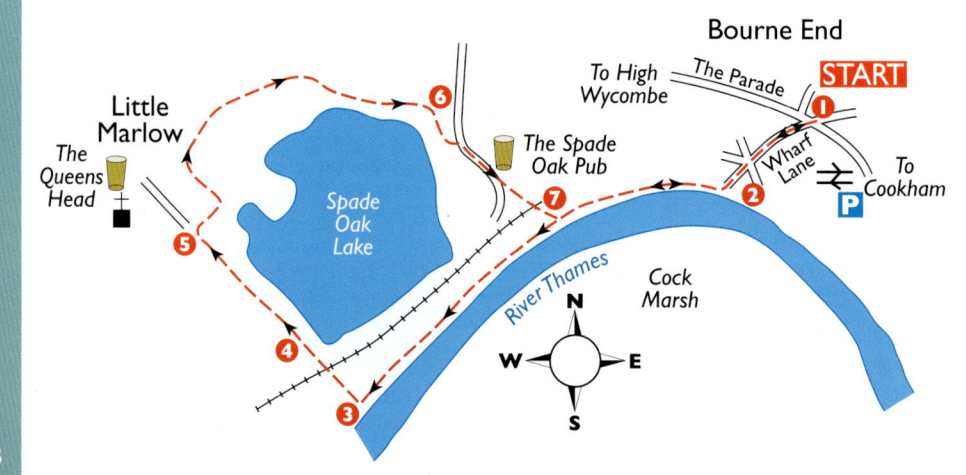

88

# Bourne End and Spade Oak Lake    19

*winter*

*Looking across the Thames towards Cock Marsh.*

**③** Now you leave the river for a while and turn right, following the hedgerow and crossing the railway track with care, bringing you to **Spade Oak Lake**.

**④** There are two parallel footpaths and, if there hasn't been too much rain recently, the best path for spotting waterbirds is the one right next to the water's edge. Continue in the same direction, crossing a private road by some cottages.

**⑤** Continuing along this road will take you into **Little Marlow**, first passing **St John the Baptist church** in front of the tiny village green, with the **Queens Head** the first turning on the left.

Otherwise, about 100m past the cottages, turn right to follow the public footpath. Cross two footbridges then turn right to follow the lane. Look out for a post, where you turn right along the public footpath to the lake. Now walk by the water again until you come to a footbridge where you turn left.

# THE CHILTERNS  Year Round Walks

**6** Cross the footbridge and through a metal gate, heading away from the lake and across a field. Then walk through a swing gate to a lane and the **Spade Oak** pub. Turn right past the pub and follow the signed footpath on the left. Follow this path back along **Upper Thames Way**, crossing back over the train track with care until you come to the river.

**7** Then turn left to retrace your steps, turning left up **Wharf Lane** into **Bourne End**.

## What to look out for –

**Spade Oak Lake** was once a quarry site, with gravel extracted from here used to make the M4. Now it's the perfect spot for observing waterbirds as they enjoy the shallow margins of this willow-fringed lake. Our milder wetlands provide a welcome retreat for migratory birds, including teals and wigeons, gulls and geese, escaping frozen continental Europe. In the summer, breeding birds include little ringed plover, reed warblers, great-crested grebes and terns. There are information boards dotted round the lake, with photos to help you identify the birds. There are also signs warning you not to swim as the water in gravel pits is always much colder than in lakes and rivers.

*Winter woods highlight the shape and form of the trees.*

*winter*

# 20 Christmas Common

### 3 miles / 4.8km

Everything about a walk at Christmas Common on a crisp winter's day makes perfect sense. The small village perched high on the Chiltern Hills derived its name from the holly trees which naturally grow in the area. Now there is a Christmas tree farm here, keeping the festive connection alive. The woodland paths are easy to navigate and the trees give good shelter from the wind. The second half of this walk follows a sunken path, dating back to Saxon times. People once used these ancient routes to travel through the landscape, as farmers took their animals to market, woodsmen hauled timber to the villages, and merchants travelled between settlements selling

# THE CHILTERNS  Year Round Walks

> **Terrain**  The start of this walk is easy walking along woodland paths. The first half of the walk goes downhill, with a steep section in the middle, then an uphill return. However, if you wanted a shorter, more level option, there is a shortcut marked on the map that halves the walk.
>
> **Map**  OS Explorer 171 Chiltern Hills West.
>
> **Starting point**  The Fox and Hounds pub. (GR SU 714931).
>
> **How to get there & parking**  Christmas Common is seven miles south of Thame. From the M40, take exit 5. The pub is just past the crossroads, as you head south through the village on the Nettlebed Road, and there is parking opposite the pub. **Sat nav:** OX49 5HN.
>
> **Refreshments**  The Fox and Hounds serves food every day. It has a lovely garden and welcomes dogs in the bar area (topfoxpub.co.uk).

their wares. At the end of the walk you can reward yourself with one of the loveliest pubs in the Chilterns. The Fox and Hounds has a series of cosy rooms and log fires to welcome walkers and their dogs, and serves delicious food.

## The Walk

**1** With your back to the pub, turn left and walk up to the crossroads. Take the right down **Hollandridge Lane**, then follow the restricted byway sign. Pass cottages on your left and fields on your right. Ignore the first footpath, then opposite the entrance to **Queen Wood Farm**, turn left to follow the bridleway signed '**Oxfordshire Way**'.

**2** Follow the bridleway through **Queen Wood**, ignoring side tracks and looking out for the white arrows painted on the trees.
 After about a mile, you come to a path on your right, heading almost back in the same direction. This path will lead you to point 6, avoiding the steeper part of the walk.

**3** Stay on the main path until you come to a bridleway.

**4** Turn right and walk steeply uphill to the edge of the wood. Then follow the path towards **Hollandridge Farm**, passing the farmhouse on your left.

# Christmas Common 20

*winter*

*Painted white arrows on the trees are perfect for keeping you on the right track.*

# THE CHILTERNS Year Round Walks

*winter*

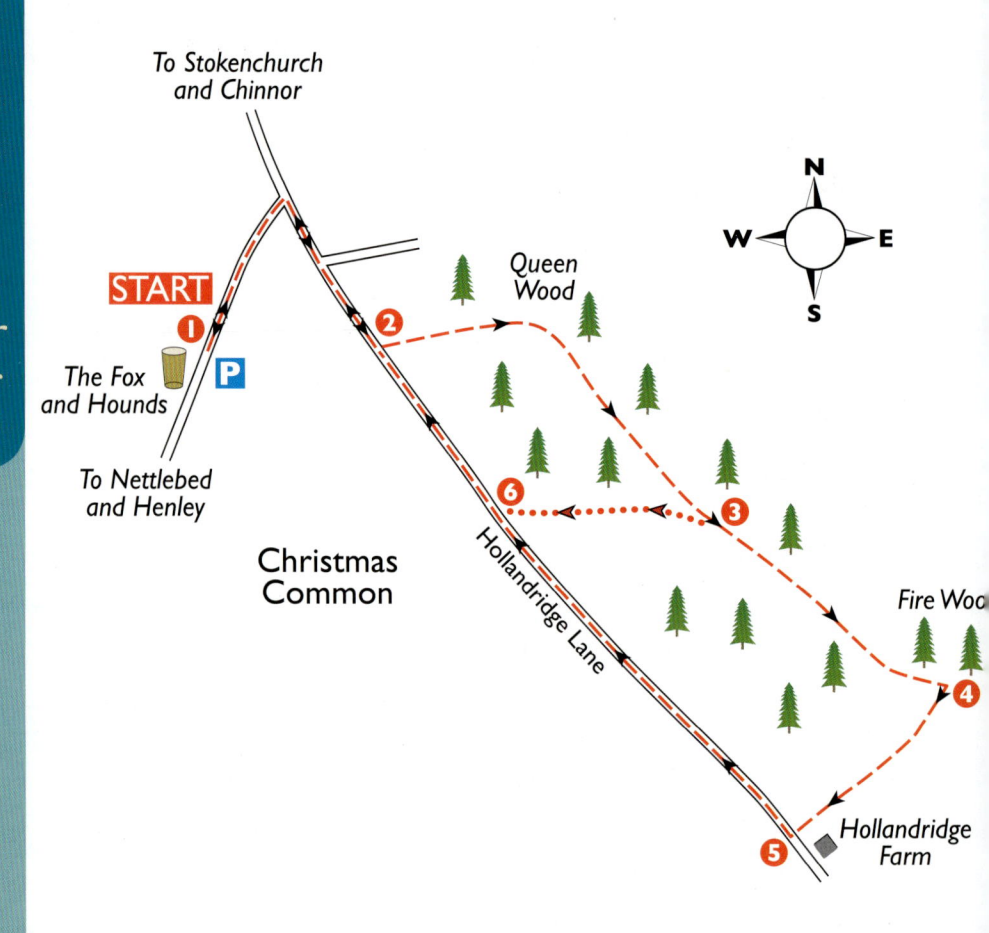

**5** You are now back on **Hollandridge Lane**. Turn right and walk up the sunken lane, and back into Queen Wood.

**6** Keep on the track until you reach the crossroads, then turn left to return to the **Fox and Hounds** pub.

## Christmas Common

### What to look out for –

*winter*

Woodland birds are easier to hear than see, and one of the pleasures of walking through woods is being surrounded by the sound of birdsong. Woods provide birds with shelter, food and nesting sites, and in winter the bare trees can make it easier to spot wildlife. The chiffchaff is easy to identify as it got its name from its characteristic song, which sounds like it is telling you its name. They used to migrate over winter and return in spring, but increasingly chiffchaffs are now overwintering. The distinctive drumming of the woodpecker is created by its hitting the tree branches with its bill. In early spring, you can hear the woodpeckers as they try to attract a mate. Jays bury acorns in the autumn to sustain them through the winter months, and they can sometimes be spotted hopping along the woodland floor in search of food. They also help the oak trees to spread, as they don't remember where all their acorns have been buried. These shy birds have a characteristic screeching call. The country's favourite bird is the robin, and they have successfully made their home in woods, hedgerows, parks and gardens, although you won't normally see two together, as these friendly little birds are in fact very aggressively territorial.

# OTHER TITLES FROM COUNTRYSIDE BOOKS

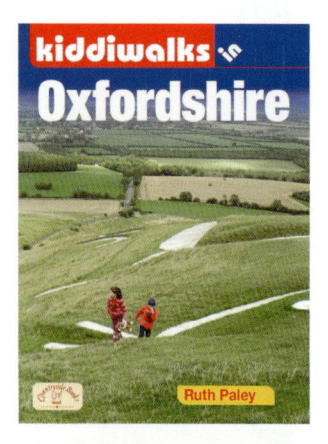

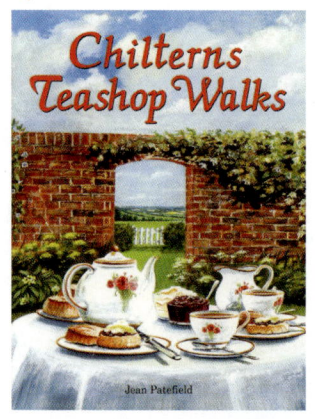

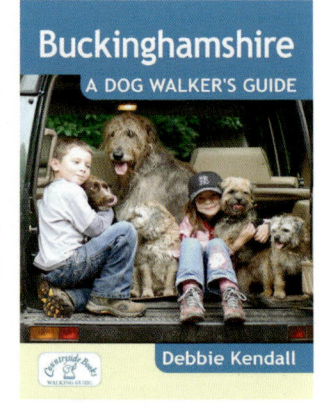

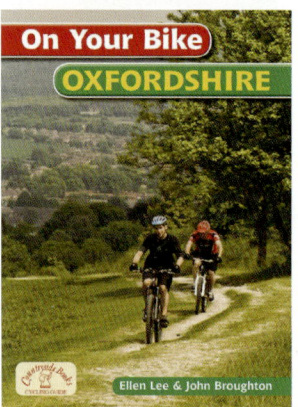

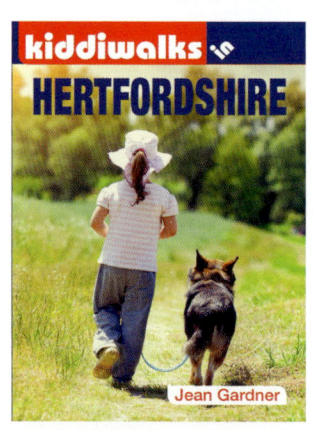

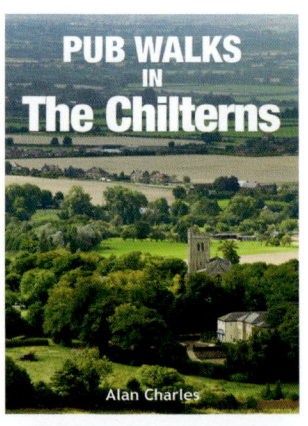

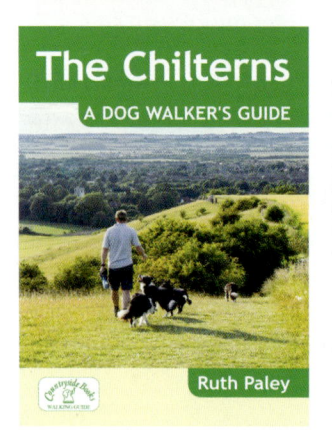

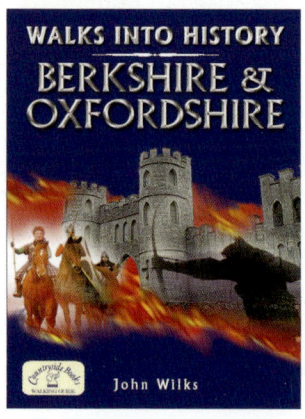

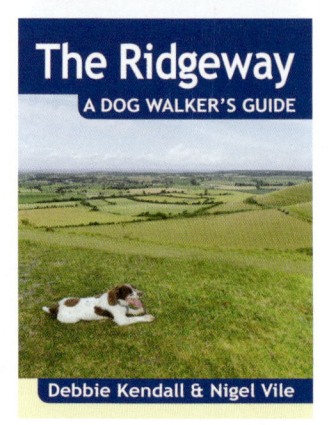

**kiddiwalks in Oxfordshire** — Ruth Paley

**Chilterns Teashop Walks** — Jean Patefield

**Buckinghamshire: A Dog Walker's Guide** — Debbie Kendall

**On Your Bike Oxfordshire** — Ellen Lee & John Broughton

**kiddiwalks in Hertfordshire** — Jean Gardner

**Pub Walks in The Chilterns** — Alan Charles

**The Chilterns: A Dog Walker's Guide** — Ruth Paley

**Walks into History: Berkshire & Oxfordshire** — John Wilks

**The Ridgeway: A Dog Walker's Guide** — Debbie Kendall & Nigel Vile

To see the full range of books by Countryside Books visit
**www.countrysidebooks.co.uk**

Follow us on [f] @CountrysideBooks